California
HMH SCIENCE DIMENSIONS™

Volume 3

Grade 8
Units 6–7

Watch the cover come alive as you explore the solar system.
Download the HMH Science Dimensions AR app available on Android or iOS devices.

This Write-In Book belongs to

_____

Teacher/Room

_____

© Houghton Mifflin Harcourt Publishing Company

Houghton Mifflin Harcourt™

Consulting Authors

Michael A. DiSpezio

Global Educator
North Falmouth,
Massachusetts

Michael DiSpezio has authored many HMH instructional programs for Science and Mathematics. He has also authored numerous trade books and multimedia programs on various topics and hosted dozens of studio and location broadcasts for various organizations in the United States and worldwide. Most recently, he has been working with educators to provide strategies for implementing the Next Generation Science Standards, particularly the Science and Engineering Practices, Crosscutting Concepts, and the use of Evidence Notebooks. To all his projects, he brings his extensive background in science, his expertise in classroom teaching at the elementary, middle, and high school levels, and his deep experience in producing interactive and engaging instructional materials.

Marjorie Frank

Science Writer and Content-
Area Reading Specialist
Brooklyn, New York

An educator and linguist by training, a writer and poet by nature, Marjorie Frank has authored and designed a generation of instructional materials in all subject areas, including past HMH Science programs. Her other credits include authoring science issues of an award-winning children's magazine, writing game-based digital assessments, developing blended learning materials for young children, and serving as instructional designer and coauthor of pioneering school-to-work software. In addition, she has served on the adjunct faculty of Hunter, Manhattan, and Brooklyn Colleges, teaching courses in science methods, literacy, and writing. For *California HMH Science Dimensions™*, she has guided the development of our K–2 strands and our approach to making connections between NGSS and Common Core ELA/literacy standards.

Acknowledgments

Cover credits: (telescope) ©HMH; (Mars) ©Stocktrek Images, Inc./Alamy.

Section Header Master Art: (machinations) ©DNY59/E+/Getty Images; (rivers on top of Greenland ice sheet) ©Maria-José Viñas, NASA Earth Science News Team; (human cells, illustration) ©Sebastian Kaulitzki/Science Photo Library/Corbis; (waves) ©Alfred Pasieka/Science Source

Printed in the U.S.A.

ISBN 978-0-358-22125-8

2 3 4 5 6 7 8 9 10 0877   27 26 25 24 23 22 21 20 19

4500759205   B C D E F G

© Houghton Mifflin Harcourt Publishing Company • Image Credits: ©HMH

Michael R. Heithaus, PhD

Dean, College of Arts, Sciences & Education Professor, Department of Biological Sciences
Florida International University
Miami, Florida

Mike Heithaus joined the FIU Biology Department in 2003 and has served as Director of the Marine Sciences Program and Executive Director of the School of Environment, Arts, and Society, which brings together the natural and social sciences and humanities to develop solutions to today's environmental challenges. He now serves as Dean of the College of Arts, Sciences & Education. His research focuses on predator-prey interactions and the ecological importance of large marine species. He has helped to guide the development of Life Science content in *California HMH Science Dimensions™*, with a focus on strategies for teaching challenging content as well as the science and engineering practices of analyzing data and using computational thinking.

Bernadine Okoro

Access and Equity Consultant

S.T.E.M. Learning Advocate & Consultant
Washington, DC

Bernadine Okoro is a chemical engineer by training and a playwright, novelist, director, and actress by nature. Okoro went from working with patents and biotechnology to teaching in K–12 classrooms. A 12-year science educator and Albert Einstein Distinguished Fellow, Okoro was one of the original authors of the Next Generation Science Standards. As a member of the Diversity and Equity Team, her focus on Alternative Education and Community Schools and on Integrating Social-Emotional Learning and Brain-Based Learning into NGSS is the vehicle she uses as a pathway to support underserved groups from elementary school to adult education. An article and book reviewer for NSTA and other educational publishing companies, Okoro currently works as a S.T.E.M. Learning Advocate & Consultant.

Cary I. Sneider, PhD

Associate Research Professor
Portland State University
Portland, Oregon

While studying astrophysics at Harvard, Cary Sneider volunteered to teach in an Upward Bound program and discovered his real calling as a science teacher. After teaching middle and high school science in Maine, California, Costa Rica, and Micronesia, he settled for nearly three decades at Lawrence Hall of Science in Berkeley, California, where he developed skills in curriculum development and teacher education. Over his career, Cary directed more than 20 federal, state, and foundation grant projects and was a writing team leader for the Next Generation Science Standards. He has been instrumental in ensuring *California HMH Science Dimensions™* meets the high expectations of the NGSS and provides an effective three-dimensional learning experience for all students.

Program Advisors

Paul D. Asimow, PhD
Eleanor and John R. McMillan
Professor of Geology and
Geochemistry
California Institute of Technology
Pasadena, California

Joanne Bourgeois
Professor Emerita
Earth & Space Sciences
University of Washington
Seattle, WA

Dr. Eileen Cashman
Professor
Humboldt State University
Arcata, California

Elizabeth A. De Stasio, PhD
Raymond J. Herzog Professor of
Science
Lawrence University
Appleton, Wisconsin

Perry Donham, PhD
Lecturer
Boston University
Boston, Massachusetts

Shila Garg, PhD
Professor Emerita of Physics
Former Dean of Faculty & Provost
The College of Wooster
Wooster, Ohio

Tatiana A. Krivosheev, PhD
Professor of Physics
Clayton State University
Morrow, Georgia

Mark B. Moldwin, PhD
Professor of Space Sciences and
Engineering
University of Michigan
Ann Arbor, Michigan

Ross H. Nehm
Stony Brook University (SUNY)
Stony Brook, NY

Kelly Y. Neiles, PhD
Assistant Professor of Chemistry
St. Mary's College of Maryland
St. Mary's City, Maryland

John Nielsen-Gammon, PhD
Regents Professor
Department of Atmospheric
Sciences
Texas A&M University
College Station, Texas

Dr. Sten Odenwald
Astronomer
NASA Goddard Spaceflight Center
Greenbelt, Maryland

Bruce W. Schafer
Executive Director
Oregon Robotics Tournament &
Outreach Program
Beaverton, Oregon

Barry A. Van Deman
President and CEO
Museum of Life and Science
Durham, North Carolina

Kim Withers, PhD
Assistant Professor
Texas A&M University-Corpus
Christi
Corpus Christi, Texas

Adam D. Woods, PhD
Professor
California State University,
Fullerton
Fullerton, California

English Development Advisors

Mercy D. Momary
Local District Northwest
Los Angeles, California

Michelle Sullivan
Balboa Elementary
San Diego, California

Lab Safety Reviewer

Kenneth R. Roy, Ph.D.
Senior Lab Safety Compliance Consultant
National Safety Consultants, LLC
Vernon, Connecticut

Classroom Reviewers & Hands-On Activities Advisors

Julie Arreola
Sun Valley Magnet School
Sun Valley, California

Pamela Bluestein
Sycamore Canyon School
Newbury Park, California

Andrea Brown
HLPUSD Science & STEAM TOSA
Hacienda Heights, California

Stephanie Greene
Science Department Chair
Sun Valley Magnet School
Sun Valley, California

Rana Mujtaba Khan
Will Rogers High School
Van Nuys, California

Suzanne Kirkhope
Willow Elementary and Round
Meadow Elementary
Agoura Hills, California

George Kwong
Schafer Park Elementary
Hayward, California

Imelda Madrid
Bassett St. Elementary School
Lake Balboa, California

Susana Martinez O'Brien
Diocese of San Diego
San Diego, California

Craig Moss
Mt. Gleason Middle School
Sunland, California

Isabel Souto
Schafer Park Elementary
Hayward, California

Emily R.C.G. Williams
South Pasadena Middle School
South Pasadena, California

VOLUME 1

UNIT 1 Energy, Forces, and Collisions

1

© Houghton Mifflin Harcourt Publishing Company • Image Credits: ©Earl Roberge/Science Source

At a hydroelectric power plant, forces help convert the energy of falling water into electrical energy.

During thunderstorms, electric charges build up within clouds to produce spectacular lightning displays.

© Houghton Mifflin Harcourt Publishing Company • Image Credits: ©DeepDesertPhoto/RooM/Getty Images

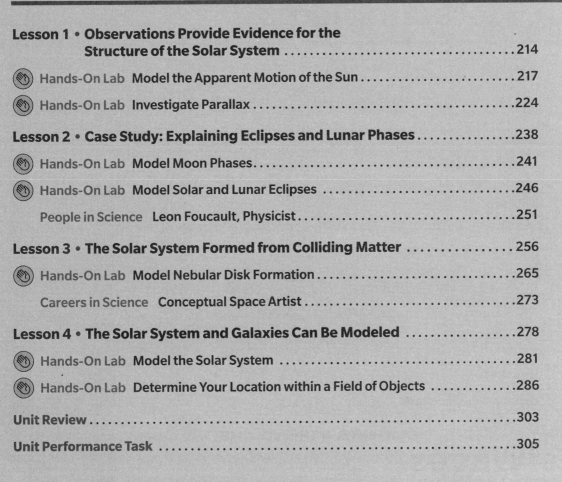
© Houghton Mifflin Harcourt Publishing Company • Image Credits: (t) ©NASA EPIC team; (b) ©Maria Stenzel/National Geographic/Getty Images

© Houghton Mifflin Harcourt Publishing Company • Image Credits: (t) ©Layne Kennedy/Corbis Documentary/Getty Images; (b) ©Willyam Bradberry/Shutterstock

© Houghton Mifflin Harcourt Publishing Company • Image Credits: ©Michael Szönyi/imageBROKER/Alamy

Ecosystem health and services are related to the biodiversity of the ecosystem.

Claims, Evidence, and Reasoning

Constructing an Argument

Constructing a strong argument is useful in science and engineering and in everyday life. A strong argument has three parts: a claim, evidence, and reasoning. Scientists and engineers use claims-evidence-reasoning arguments to communicate their explanations and solutions to others and to challenge or debate the conclusions of other scientists and engineers. The words *argue* and *argument* do not mean that scientists or engineers are fighting about something. Instead, this is a way to support a claim using evidence. Argumentation is a calm and rational way for people to examine all the facts and come to the best conclusion.

A **claim** is a statement that answers the question "What do you know?" A claim is a statement of your understanding of a phenomenon, answer to a question, or solution to a problem. A claim states what you think is true based on the information you have.

Evidence is any data that are related to your claim and answer the question "How do you know that?" These data may be from your own experiments and observations, reports by scientists or engineers, or other reliable data. Arguments made in science and engineering should be supported by empirical evidence. Empirical evidence is evidence that comes from observation or experiment.

Evidence used to support a claim should also be relevant and sufficient. Relevant evidence is evidence that is about the claim, and not about something else. Evidence is sufficient when there is enough evidence to fully support the claim.

Reasoning is the use of logical, analytical thought to form conclusions or inferences. Reasoning answers the question "Why does your evidence support your claim?" So, reasoning explains the relationship between your evidence and your claim. Reasoning might include a scientific law or principle that helps explain the relationship between the evidence and the claim.

© Houghton Mifflin Harcourt Publishing Company • Image Credits: ©HMH

Here is an example of a claims-evidence-reasoning argument.

Claim	Ice melts faster in the sun than it does in the shade.
Evidence	Two ice cubes of the same size were each placed in a plastic dish. One dish was placed on a wooden bench in the sun and one was placed on a different part of the same bench in the shade. The ice cube in the sun melted in 14 minutes and 32 seconds. The ice cube in the shade melted in 18 minutes and 15 seconds.
Reasoning	This experiment was designed so that the only variable that was different in the set-up of the two ice cubes was whether they were in the shade or in the sun. Because the ice cube in the sun melted almost 4 minutes faster than the one in the shade, this is sufficient evidence to say that ice melts faster in the sun than it does in the shade.

To summarize, a strong argument:

- presents a claim that is clear, logical, and well-defended
- supports the claim with empirical evidence that is sufficient and relevant
- includes reasons that make sense and are presented in a logical order

Constructing Your Own Argument

Now construct your own argument by recording a claim, evidence, and reasoning. With your teacher's permission, you can do an investigation to answer a question you have about how the world works. Or you can construct your argument based on observations you have already made about the world.

Claim	
Evidence	
Reasoning	

 For more information on claims, evidence, and reasoning, see the online **English Language Arts Handbook.**

Whether you are in the lab or in the field, you are responsible for your own safety and the safety of others. To fulfill these responsibilities and avoid accidents, be aware of the safety of your classmates as well as your own safety at all times. Take your lab work and fieldwork seriously, and behave appropriately. Elements of safety to keep in mind are shown below and on the following pages.

Safety in the Lab

☐ Be sure you understand the materials, your procedure, and the safety rules before you start an investigation in the lab.

☐ Know where to find and how to use fire extinguishers, eyewash stations, shower stations, and emergency power shutoffs.

☐ Use proper safety equipment. Always wear personal protective equipment, such as eye protection and gloves, when setting up labs, during labs, and when cleaning up.

☐ Do not begin until your teacher has told you to start. Follow directions.

☐ Keep the lab neat and uncluttered. Clean up when you are finished. Report all spills to your teacher immediately. Watch for slip/fall and trip/fall hazards.

☐ If you or another student is injured in any way, tell your teacher immediately, even if the injury seems minor.

☐ Do not take any food or drink into the lab. Never take any chemicals out of the lab.

Safety in the Field

☐ Be sure you understand the goal of your fieldwork and the proper way to carry out the investigation before you begin fieldwork.

☐ Use proper safety equipment and personal protective equipment, such as eye protection, that suits the terrain and the weather.

☐ Follow directions, including appropriate safety procedures as provided by your teacher.

☐ Do not approach or touch wild animals. Do not touch plants unless instructed by your teacher to do so. Leave natural areas as you found them.

☐ Stay with your group.

☐ Use proper accident procedures, and let your teacher know about a hazard in the environment or an accident immediately, even if the hazard or accident seems minor.

Safety Symbols

To highlight specific types of precautions, the following symbols are used throughout the lab program. Remember that no matter what safety symbols you see within each lab, all safety rules should be followed at all times.

Dress Code

- Wear safety goggles (or safety glasses as appropriate for the activity) at all times in the lab as directed. If chemicals get into your eye, flush your eyes immediately for a minimum of 15 minutes.
- Do not wear contact lenses in the lab.
- Do not look directly at the sun or any intense light source or laser.
- Wear appropriate protective non-latex gloves as directed.
- Wear an apron or lab coat at all times in the lab as directed.
- Tie back long hair, secure loose clothing, and remove loose jewelry. Remove acrylic nails when working with active flames.
- Do not wear open-toed shoes, sandals, or canvas shoes in the lab.

Glassware and Sharp Object Safety

- Do not use chipped or cracked glassware.
- Use heat-resistant glassware for heating or storing hot materials.
- Notify your teacher immediately if a piece of glass breaks.
- Use extreme care when handling any sharp or pointed instruments.
- Do not cut an object while holding the object unsupported in your hands. Place the object on a suitable cutting surface, and always cut in a direction away from your body.

Chemical Safety

- If a chemical gets on your skin, on your clothing, or in your eyes, rinse it immediately for a minimum of 15 minutes (using the shower, faucet, or eyewash station), and alert your teacher.
- Do not clean up spilled chemicals unless your teacher directs you to do so.
- Do not inhale any gas or vapor unless directed to do so by your teacher. If you are instructed to note the odor of a substance, wave the fumes toward your nose with your hand. This is called wafting. Never put your nose close to the source of the odor.
- Handle materials that emit vapors or gases in a well-ventilated area.
- Keep your hands away from your face while you are working on any activity.

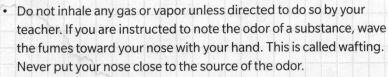

Safety Symbols, continued

Electrical Safety

- Do not use equipment with frayed electrical cords or loose plugs.
- Do not use electrical equipment near water or when clothing or hands are wet.
- Hold the plug housing when you plug in or unplug equipment. Do not pull on the cord.
- Use only GFI-protected electrical receptacles.

Heating and Fire Safety

- Be aware of any source of flames, sparks, or heat (such as flames, heating coils, or hot plates) before working with any flammable substances.
- Know the location of the lab's fire extinguisher and fire-safety blankets.
- Know your school's fire-evacuation routes.
- If your clothing catches on fire, walk to the lab shower to put out the fire. Do not run.
- Never leave a hot plate unattended while it is turned on or while it is cooling.
- Use tongs or appropriately insulated holders when handling heated objects.
- Allow all equipment to cool before storing it.

Plant and Animal Safety

- Do not eat any part of a plant.
- Do not pick any wild plant unless your teacher instructs you to do so.
- Handle animals only as your teacher directs.
- Treat animals carefully and respectfully.
- Wash your hands thoroughly with soap and water after handling any plant or animal.

Cleanup

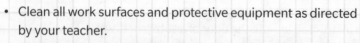

- Clean all work surfaces and protective equipment as directed by your teacher.
- Dispose of hazardous materials or sharp objects only as directed by your teacher.
- Wash your hands thoroughly with soap and water before you leave the lab or after any activity.

Student Safety Quiz

Circle the letter of the BEST answer.

1. Before starting an investigation or lab procedure, you should
   - **A.** try an experiment of your own
   - **B.** open all containers and packages
   - **C.** read all directions and make sure you understand them
   - **D.** handle all the equipment to become familiar with it

2. At the end of any activity you should
   - **A.** wash your hands thoroughly with soap and water before leaving the lab
   - **B.** cover your face with your hands
   - **C.** put on your safety goggles
   - **D.** leave hot plates switched on

3. If you get hurt or injured in any way, you should
   - **A.** tell your teacher immediately
   - **B.** find bandages or a first aid kit
   - **C.** go to your principal's office
   - **D.** get help after you finish the lab

4. If your glassware is chipped or broken, you should
   - **A.** use it only for solid materials
   - **B.** give it to your teacher for recycling or disposal
   - **C.** put it back into the storage cabinet
   - **D.** increase the damage so that it is obvious

5. If you have unused chemicals after finishing a procedure, you should
   - **A.** pour them down a sink or drain
   - **B.** mix them all together in a bucket
   - **C.** put them back into their original containers
   - **D.** dispose of them as directed by your teacher

6. If electrical equipment has a frayed cord, you should
   - **A.** unplug the equipment by pulling the cord
   - **B.** let the cord hang over the side of a counter or table
   - **C.** tell your teacher about the problem immediately
   - **D.** wrap tape around the cord to repair it

7. If you need to determine the odor of a chemical or a solution, you should
   - **A.** use your hand to bring fumes from the container to your nose
   - **B.** bring the container under your nose and inhale deeply
   - **C.** tell your teacher immediately
   - **D.** use odor-sensing equipment

8. When working with materials that might fly into the air and hurt someone's eye, you should wear
   - **A.** goggles
   - **B.** an apron
   - **C.** gloves
   - **D.** a hat

9. Before doing experiments involving a heat source, you should know the location of the
   - **A.** door
   - **B.** window
   - **C.** fire extinguisher
   - **D.** overhead lights

10. If you get chemicals in your eye you should
    - **A.** wash your hands immediately
    - **B.** put the lid back on the chemical container
    - **C.** wait to see if your eye becomes irritated
    - **D.** use the eyewash station right away, for a minimum of 15 minutes

Go online to view the Lab Safety Handbook for additional information.

Waves

How are waves and energy related to Earth's seasons?

Dolphins are at home swimming through waves in the ocean. They communicate with each other using sound waves that travel through water or air. They can even use sound waves to find food.

You Solve It How Can We Harvest Energy from Ocean Waves?
Use a model wave power generator to analyze how wave characteristics affect the generation of electrical energy. Choose a location for a wave energy farm.

Go online and complete the You Solve It to explore ways to solve a real-world problem.

Design Wave Interactions

A person wears hearing protection as he inspects an airplane on the tarmac at an airport.

A. Look at the photo. On a separate sheet of paper, write down as many different questions as you can about the photo.

B. **Discuss** With your class or a partner, share your questions. Record any additional questions generated in your discussion. Then choose the most important questions from the list that are related to minimizing the effect of a wave on humans. Write them below.

C. Make a list of as many different wave types as you can. From the list, identify which types that you or other people interact with and how you interact with the wave. Then choose which interaction you want to research.

D. Use the information above, along with your research, to design a method to minimize the effect of the wave on a person.

Discuss the next steps for your Unit Project with your teacher and go online to download the Unit Project Worksheet.

Language Development

Use the lessons in this unit to complete the network and expand your understanding of these key concepts.

	Similar term
	Phrase
	Cognate
	Example
	Definition

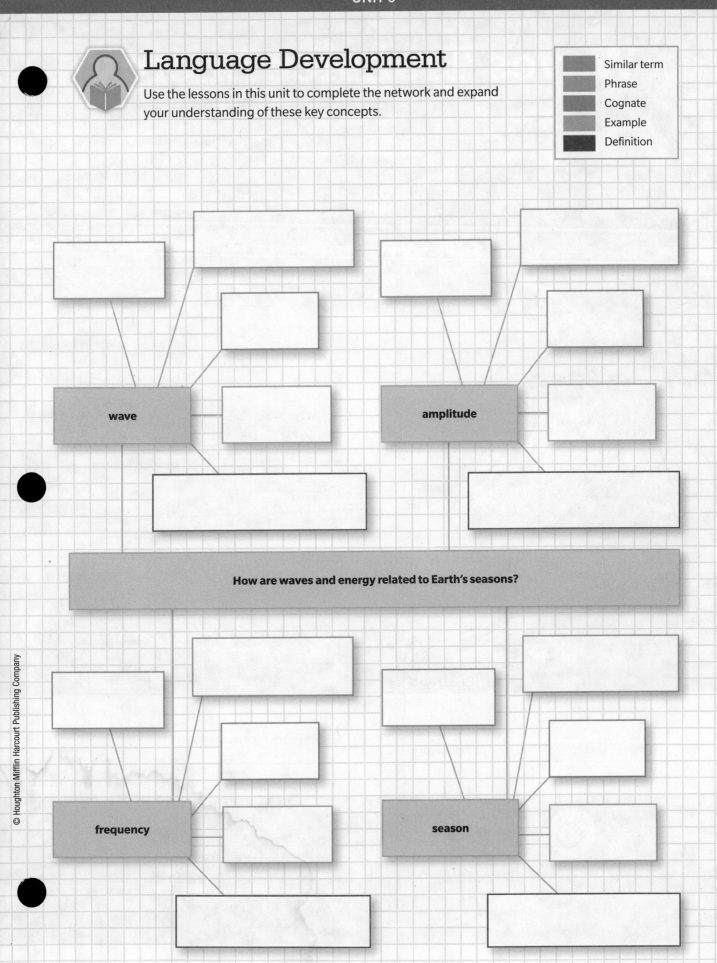

wave

amplitude

How are waves and energy related to Earth's seasons?

frequency

season

Waves Transfer Energy

Ocean waves can be described by the same properties as some other kinds of waves.

© Houghton Mifflin Harcourt Publishing Company • Image Credits: ©Willyam Bradberry/Shutterstock

 Explore First

Exploring Vibrations Tap lightly on one side of an inflated balloon with a stick or unsharpened pencil while a partner places their ear on the other side of the balloon. Trade places and repeat the tapping. What did you notice? Work with your partner to develop an explanation for what you observed.

Go online to view the digital version of the Hands-On Lab for this lesson and to download additional lab resources.

CAN YOU EXPLAIN IT?

How do falling dominoes compare to a wave?

The person in the picture transfers energy from himself to the first domino, which causes the rest of the dominoes to fall.

Explore Online

1. How does the energy from the person's hand get to the last domino?

EVIDENCE NOTEBOOK As you explore the lesson, gather evidence to help explain how the falling dominoes are similar to and different from a wave.

Exploring Waves

Water crashing onshore, the spotlight on center stage, and a siren blaring may seem unrelated, but they have one thing in common—waves. The world is full of waves, including water waves, light waves, and sound waves.

When a swimmer jumps into a pool, he does not just make a big splash. He also causes waves to spread through the water in the pool.

2. Think about the energy that was needed to form a wave in the pool. Where did the energy come from?

Waves and Energy

A water wave is just one kind of wave. A **wave** is a repeating disturbance that transfers energy from one place to another. A wave transfers energy in the direction that the wave travels. In the diagram of the insect on water, the wave travels to the right, so energy is transferred to the right. How much energy is transferred depends on the size of the disturbance. The greater the disturbance is, the more energy is transferred. However, a wave does not transfer matter. The matter in which a wave travels, called the **medium**, does not move along with it. The plural of medium is media. Waves can be complex, but a lot can be learned by studying simple waves.

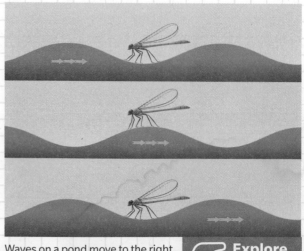

Waves on a pond move to the right, but the insect only bobs up and down due to a small disturbance.

Explore Online

3. Look at the wave traveling through the rope. The left end of the rope is being shaken, so the wave is traveling to the right / left . The energy of the wave travels to the right / left along the rope. As the wave goes by, each piece of the rope moves up and down / along with the wave .

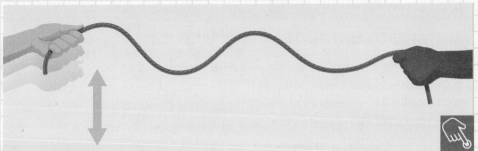

The points on the rope vibrate perpendicularly, or at a right angle, to the direction that the wave moves.

Waves and Wave Pulses

As a wave travels, energy is transferred. If the wave's energy is transferred only one time, then a wave *pulse* is formed. You can see a single pulse as it moves through the medium. If the disturbance transfers energy in a repeating pattern, then a wave is formed and you can see the wave moving continuously.

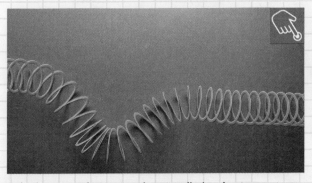

A single wave pulse moves along a coiled spring toy.

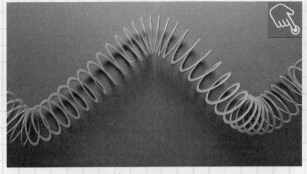

Repeating wave pulses form a wave in a coiled spring toy.

4. Discuss Together with a partner, look at the two photos and compare your observations. What wave patterns do you observe? Think about how the wave patterns are similar and how they are different and summarize your conclusions.

5. Which properties of waves discussed so far do the dominoes exhibit? Record your evidence.

Compare a Tsunami to Smaller Water Waves

Waves can be different sizes and shapes, and they can transfer different amounts of energy. A tsunami is a large ocean wave caused by a disturbance in or around the sea, such as an underwater earthquake. A large amount of energy is needed to generate such a large wave, and a tsunami can cause a lot of destruction once it reaches land.

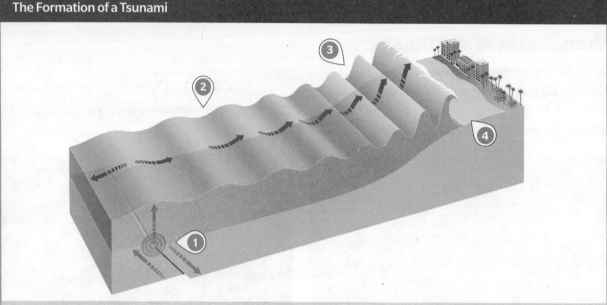

The Formation of a Tsunami

1. An underwater fault in the ocean floor releases a massive amount of energy and displaces the water above it. Waves are formed as energy moves outward from the fault.

2. Waves build and move as fast as 800 km/h. In deep water, the waves are only 30–60 cm above sea level, but each wave pulse may be hundreds of kilometers long.

3. As the bottom of each wave pulse approaches the shoreline, the wave slows down, increases in height, and the wave pulses come closer together.

4. At the coast, the waves are at their tallest. These giant waves crash onto the shore and can cause massive damage.

6. What does a tsunami have in common with a wave generated by a person jumping into a pool?

_____

_____

_____

_____

_____

_____

_____

_____

Comparing Longitudinal and Transverse Waves

When a wave travels from one end of a rope to the other end, the parts of the rope move in a different direction from the direction that the wave travels. The parts of rope are the "particles" of the medium. In a rope wave, the particles vibrate perpendicularly to the direction that the wave travels, which makes the rope wave an example of a *transverse wave*. In another type of wave, called a *longitudinal wave*, the particles vibrate parallel to the direction that the wave travels. During an earthquake, both types of waves occur.

During an earthquake, the ground can move in dramatic ways. Powerful waves—both longitudinal and transverse waves—travel through Earth's crust.

 7. Language SmArts What type of movement do you think is responsible for the damage shown in the photo? Write a paragraph that relates the ground movement during an earthquake to wave type. Create a visual model to clarify how the waves cause damage.

Hands-On Lab
Model Two Types of Waves

Use a coiled spring toy to model two types of waves: a longitudinal wave and a transverse wave.

MATERIALS
• spring toy, coiled

Procedure

STEP 1 Hold a coiled spring toy on the floor between you and a lab partner so that the spring is straight. This is the rest position of the spring. As you do this lab, be sure to keep the spring on the floor as you move it. Another lab partner will document each step.

STEP 2 Move one end of the spring to produce a transverse wave. Describe how you moved the spring and record your observations for Wave 1.

Wave	Observations and Wave Types
Wave 1	
Wave 2	

STEP 3 Allow the spring to return to its rest position.

STEP 4 Move one end of the spring to produce a longitudinal wave. Describe how you moved the spring and record your observations for Wave 2.

Analysis

STEP 5 Discuss Together with your partners, compare the waves that you made. How are the waves alike and how are they different? What patterns did you observe? Include examples from your investigation.

Longitudinal and Transverse Waves

Both longitudinal waves and transverse waves transfer energy in the direction that they travel. However, they differ in the way the disturbances move in relation to the direction of wave motion. In a longitudinal wave, the coils move parallel to the direction that the wave travels. An area where the coils are close together is called a compression, and an area where the coils are spread out is called a rarefaction. In a transverse wave, the coils move perpendicularly to the direction that the wave travels. The highest point of the wave is called a crest, and the lowest point is called a trough.

Other types of waves exist, such as surface waves. Surface waves form at the boundary of two media and are a combination of longitudinal waves and transverse waves. Water waves and some seismic waves are examples of surface waves.

8. Label the type and parts of the waves shown in the diagrams.

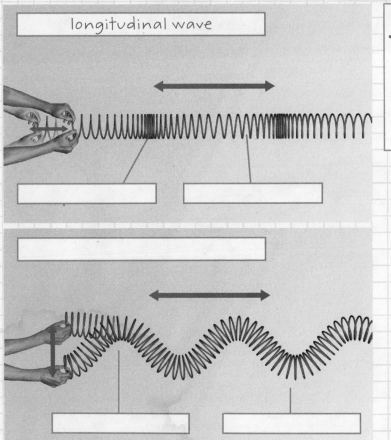

longitudinal wave

WORD BANK
- longitudinal wave
- transverse wave
- compression
- rarefaction
- crest
- trough

9. Describe the movement of the dominoes as energy is transferred through them and then compare the movement of longitudinal waves to the movement of the dominoes. Record your evidence.

Analyze the Types of Waves in Earthquakes

Earthquakes produce both longitudinal waves and transverse waves that travel through Earth's crust. Longitudinal waves and transverse waves often travel at different speeds in a medium. During earthquakes, longitudinal waves are faster, and they arrive first during an earthquake. The transverse waves, which are slower but usually more destructive, arrive seconds later.

10. The arrows in the diagrams show the direction that the seismic waves are traveling. Label the diagrams as either a longitudinal wave or a transverse wave.

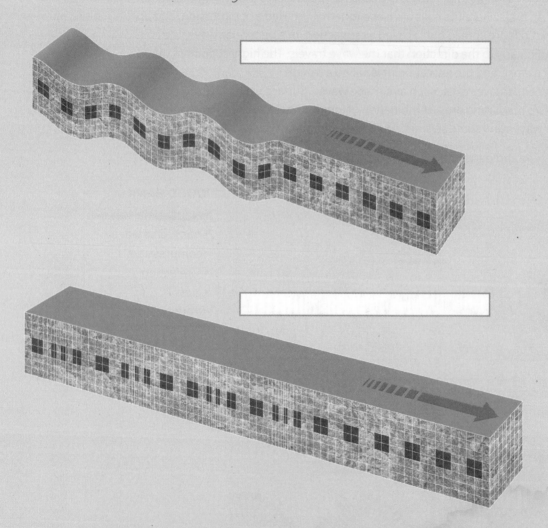

11. If you see the ground moving forward and backward during an earthquake, then you are probably experiencing a longitudinal / transverse wave. If you see the ground moving up and down, then it is likely a longitudinal / transverse wave. In both cases, matter / energy is transferred.

Identifying the Properties of Waves

Picture it: It is a calm day on a quiet street, and a car pulls up to the curb and parks. The driver gets out of the car, pulls down his hat to hide his face, and hurries away. Suddenly, the car explodes!

Fortunately, this violent explosion is part of a scene from a movie. The explosion created a blast wave; a high-pressure wave that radiates out, carrying a lot of energy from the center of the explosion. Special effects experts carefully design and carry out these types of controlled explosions, and set up situations to look like the after effects of an explosion without actually creating a blast wave.

12. A film crew is setting up a scene to show the effects of a blast wave on nearby cars. Why do you think the cars are hanging from cables?

An explosion is a high-energy event that can create a blast wave. A movie's special effects team simulates the effects of a blast wave.

Properties of Waves Can Be Modeled

Waves are described by their properties. A measure of how far a particle in the medium moves away from its normal rest position is the **amplitude**. The amplitude of a transverse wave is half of the difference between the crest and the trough and is equal to the height of the wave above the rest position. The distance from any point on a wave to an identical point on the next wave pulse is the **wavelength**. Wavelength measures the length of one cycle, or repetition, of a wave. A wave can be modeled on a graph.

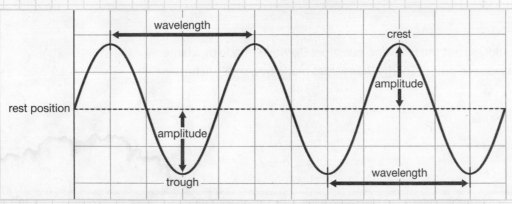

13. Discuss In a small group, discuss the wave characteristics shown in the diagram. Explain why the wavelength can be measured as the distance between consecutive peaks or consecutive troughs.

© Houghton Mifflin Harcourt Publishing Company • Image Credits: ©EuroStyle Graphics/ Alamy

Hands-On Lab
Investigate Waves

Investigate how waves in a water-filled tray affect the medium that they travel through.

MATERIALS
- block, wood, rectangular
- cork
- tray, baking, aluminum, deep
- water

Procedure and Analysis

STEP 1 Fill the tray about halfway with water. Place a cork in the water near the center of the tray.

STEP 2 Choose one group member to move the block up and down in the water at one end of the tray to produce waves. At different times, move the block up and down at different speeds.

STEP 3 Observe the motion of the cork and the water. Sketch and describe your observations.

STEP 4 What is the relationship between the energy of the wave you created in Step 2 and the speed at which the cork moves up and down?

STEP 5 How could you test the following question: Do waves made by a large disturbance carry more energy than waves made by a small disturbance?

14. Collaborate With a partner, develop an informational pamphlet that teaches a student how to graph the properties of a wave. You may use any wave type in your examples.

Frequency and Speed of a Wave

Think about the water waves that you made. The cork bobbed up and down more or less quickly, depending on how quickly you moved the block. The number of wave pulses produced in a set amount of time is the **frequency** of the wave. Frequency is usually expressed in *hertz* (Hz), and for waves, one hertz equals one wave pulse per second (1 Hz = 1/s). The rate at which a wave travels is *wave speed*, which can be calculated by multiplying wavelength and frequency. The equation for wave speed (*v*) is $v = \lambda \times f$, where wavelength is λ and frequency is f. For example, to determine the wave speed of a wave that has a wavelength of 5 m and a frequency of 4 Hz, substitute the values given for λ and f and solve: $v = 5 \text{ m} \times 4 \text{ Hz} = 20 \text{ m/s}$.

 15. Do the Math What is the wave speed of a wave that has a wavelength of 2 m and a frequency of 6 Hz?

 16. Engineer It An engineer has been asked to give advice about a wave pool at a local water park. The park guests think that the waves in the pool are too close together. The engineer knows that the wave speed in the pool is constant. Explain why the engineer suggests reducing the frequency of the wave generator.

Energy and Amplitude of a Wave

The amplitude of a wave is dependent on energy. For example, when using a rope to make waves, you have to work harder to produce a wave that has a large amplitude than to produce one that has a small amplitude because it takes more energy to move the rope farther from its rest position. When comparing waves that have the same frequency in the same medium, the wave that has the larger amplitude carries more energy.

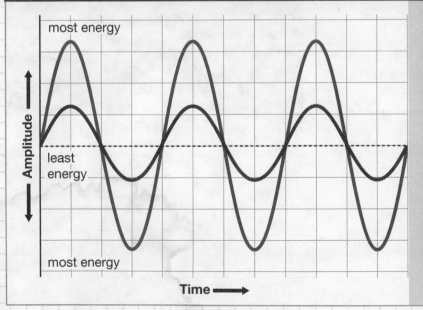

Energy Is Proportional to Amplitude

most energy

least energy

most energy

Amplitude

Time →

Lower amplitude waves are perfect for a relaxing day at the beach.

Surfers need higher amplitude waves to catch an exciting ride.

Calculate Amplitude

The relationship between amplitude and wave energy is that energy is proportional to amplitude squared. For example, if the amplitude of the waves at one beach is three times the amplitude of the waves at another beach, you might think that the taller waves have three times as much energy as the shorter waves have. However, the taller waves would actually have nine times as much energy because nine is three squared ($3^2 = 9$).

What if you started knowing energy instead? Suppose that your lab partner told you the energy of a wave increased by a factor of 16, and you want to determine how the amplitude changed. You would find that the amplitude quadrupled because the square root of 16 is equal to 4 ($\sqrt{16} = 4$). You can use the relationship between amplitude and energy to find one variable if you know the other variable.

 17. Do the Math If the energy of a wave increased by a factor of 25, by what factor did the amplitude of the wave increase?

 Language SmArts
Apply Your Knowledge of Wave Energy and Amplitude

Suppose that you are an actor in a movie in which a car explodes. It could be exciting to be next to an exploding car, but it could also be dangerous! An explosion produces a blast wave that radiates out with a lot of energy. Special effects experts have to apply their knowledge of energy and amplitude when designing explosions to keep people on the set safe during such scenes.

18. Special effects experts want the largest explosion that is safe for the people on set. Knowing that the energy of a wave is proportional to its amplitude squared helps them mathematically model the energy of the explosion and the amplitude of the blast wave. How does this knowledge help them determine where to place the actors and crew?

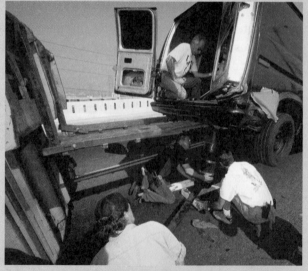

The special effects team is working to modify a vehicle for a special effect that will only last a few seconds.

_____

_____

_____

_____

_____

_____

Continue Your Exploration

Name: _____ **Date:** _____

Check out the path below or go online to choose one of the other paths shown.

> **People in Science**

> • **Earthquakes and Waves**
> • **Hands-On Labs** ✋
> • **Propose Your Own Path**

> *Go online to choose one of these other paths.*

James West, Research Scientist

James West's parents wanted him to be a medical doctor, but he wanted to study physics. His father was sure that West would never find a job in physics, but West wanted to study what he loved. He did study physics, and he did find a job. West worked for Bell Laboratories where he developed a microphone called the electret microphone. Today, versions of West's microphone are in almost all telephones, cell phones, and other equipment that record sound.

West's interest in the microphone started with a question about hearing. A group of scientists wanted to know how close together two sounds could be before the ear would not be able to tell them apart. The scientists needed a very sensitive microphone to produce the sounds for their tests, and at the time, no microphone sensitive enough existed. West and fellow scientist Dr. Gerhard Sessler found that they could make a more sensitive microphone by using materials called electrets. The new microphones were cheaper, more reliable, smaller, and lighter than any microphone before.

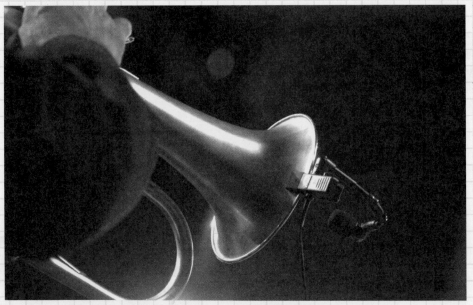

West's research into sound waves and hearing has helped make microphones smaller.

Continue Your Exploration

Microphones convert sound waves into electrical signals. The original design West and his colleagues were researching used a battery to power a material that had no electric charge, but an accident converted the uncharged material to an electret. An electret can be thought of as an electric version of a magnet. It has two oppositely charged poles. West and his colleagues began to study this new material and found that it was not only more sensitive but did not require a battery to maintain its charge. Based on this evidence, the researchers reasoned that this material could be used in more sensitive microphones. At the time, they could not have foreseen the use of this technology in cell phones, so the application was initially purely for research.

1. How does this example show that there is value in research science, even if a practical application for the science does not currently exist?

2. West has always been interested in how things work. When he was younger, he enjoyed taking apart small appliances to see what was inside. Why would curiosity about how things work be useful to a research scientist?

3. Research scientists work in all scientific disciplines. West studied physics and focused his research on sound waves. If you were a research scientist, what discipline would you be most interested in studying and what specific topics would you be interested in researching? Explain why.

4. **Collaborate** Work with a group to find a recent discovery in wave research. As a group, imagine how this discovery may lead to other applications. Share your ideas with the class.

Can You Explain It?

Name: _____   **Date:** _____

How do falling dominoes compare to a wave?

EVIDENCE NOTEBOOK

Refer to the notes in your Evidence Notebook to help you determine how falling dominoes compare to a wave.

1. State your claim. Make sure your claim fully explains how falling dominoes compare to a wave.

2. Summarize the evidence you have gathered to support your claim and explain your reasoning.

Checkpoints

Answer the following questions to check your understanding of the lesson.

Use the photo to answer Questions 3–4.

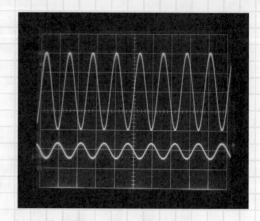

3. The upper wave has more / less energy than the bottom wave, because the amplitude / wavelength / frequency of the upper wave is greater than that of the bottom wave.

4. Look at the bottom waveform. Approximately how many wavelengths are shown?
   A. 2.5
   B. 4
   C. 8
   D. 16

Use the diagram to answer Questions 5–6.

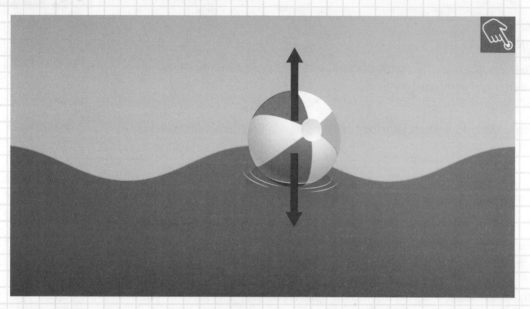

5. Which statements are true about the diagram? Select all that apply.
   A. The ball moves along with the wave as the wave moves.
   B. The ball moves up and down as the wave passes by.
   C. The wave transfers energy as it moves.
   D. The ball transfers energy to the wave.

6. Which medium is the wave traveling through?
   A. air
   B. water
   C. plastic

Interactive Review

Complete this section to review the main concepts of the lesson.

A wave is a disturbance that transfers energy from one place to another and transfers energy in the direction that it travels.

A. Explain how a wave transfers energy from one place to another.

Waves can be classified by comparing the direction of the disturbance and the direction that the wave travels.

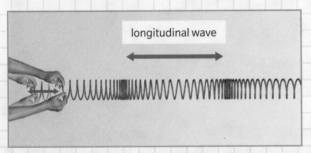

longitudinal wave

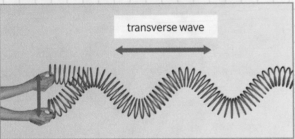

transverse wave

B. Explain the difference between longitudinal waves and transverse waves in terms of particle vibration.

The key properties of waves include amplitude, wavelength, frequency, and wave speed. Graphs can be used to model the properties of waves.

C. Use a model to explain how frequency and wavelength relate to wave speed.

Waves Interact with Matter

When a pool of water is disturbed, a wave spreads out over the surface of the water.

Explore First

Exploring Sound Gently stretch a rubber band. Then pluck the rubber band and listen to the sound that it makes. Stretch the rubber band a little more, and pluck the rubber band again. How does the vibration of the rubber band relate to how high or low the sound is?

Go online to view the digital version of the Hands-On Lab for this lesson and to download additional lab resources.

CAN YOU EXPLAIN IT?

How can features and objects on the sea floor be visualized using mechanical waves?

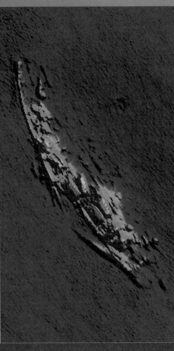

Because waves interact with matter, waves can be used to observe the world. These images were made using sound waves, a type of mechanical wave, interacting with the sea floor and objects on it.

1. What do you think the different colors in the images represent?

2. What do you see in each image?

EVIDENCE NOTEBOOK As you explore the lesson, gather evidence to help explain how mechanical waves can be used to visualize the sea floor.

Investigating Mechanical Waves

When you shout at your friend across the room, sound waves carry energy through the air. Your friend senses that energy when he or she hears your voice. The air does not move from your vocal cords to your friend's eardrum, though. The sound waves move through the air, causing the air particles to vibrate as the energy passes through them.

3. Tsunamis are often caused by underwater earthquakes. Once a tsunami forms, the wave can travel hundreds of kilometers before reaching land. Explain whether or not the water molecules that touch land are the same ones that the earthquake initially moved.

The waves that can be seen moving through water are similar to sound waves in many ways.

Mechanical Waves

Some waves, such as sound waves, require a medium through which to travel. A medium can be air, water, steel, or any other material. A *vacuum* is a volume that contains no particles of matter, so a vacuum is not a medium. A **mechanical wave** is a wave that travels through a medium due to the motion of matter. When a book is slammed on a table, it creates a disturbance in the air particles around the book. This disturbance creates a mechanical wave that moves out from the book and reaches your ear. The air is the medium that the wave traveled through, and the sound is the mechanical wave.

5. **Language SmArts** Work in small groups and have each group member select a type of wave that they are familiar with. Determine where the initial energy for the wave comes from and what medium the wave travels through, and then sketch the initial energy input and the medium of the wave. Taking turns, present each of your waves to the other members of your group.

Label the Medium

4. Label the medium that each mechanical wave is passing through.

Hands-On Lab
Generate Mechanical Waves

Generate waves in several media and observe how the mechanical waves behave.

MATERIALS
- paper strips, long
- spring toy, coiled
- string or rope
- water, in tub

Procedure and Analysis

STEP 1 Choose an object to use as a wave medium.

STEP 2 Experiment with ways to generate a mechanical wave in the medium. Note that you may find more than one way to generate waves in a particular medium.

STEP 3 Observe the waves that you generated and record your observations in the data table.

STEP 4 Repeat Steps 1–3 using other media.

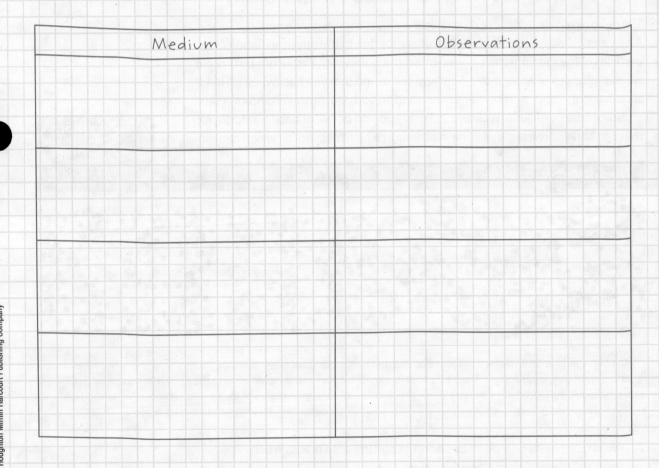

Medium	Observations

© Houghton Mifflin Harcourt Publishing Company

EVIDENCE NOTEBOOK

6. What occurred when a wave moving through the water hit the side of its container? How might this relate to using sound waves in water to visualize the sea floor? Record your evidence.

Lesson 2 Waves Interact with Matter **501**

STEP 5 Discuss Choose one of the media that you used to generate mechanical waves and identify how you can observe the amplitude, frequency, and speed of the wave as it travels through the medium.

Waves Interact with Particles of a Medium

The defining characteristic of mechanical waves is the need for a medium. A mechanical wave travels through a substance due to the physical motion of the particles of the medium itself. For example, the waves in the wake of a boat occur when molecules of water move. Similarly, the sound that you hear when a friend shouts occurs when air molecules move, and an earthquake travels through the ground as the particles of rock and soil move up and down, or back and forth. All of these materials are examples of media through which mechanical waves can move.

Explore Online

Types of Mechanical Waves

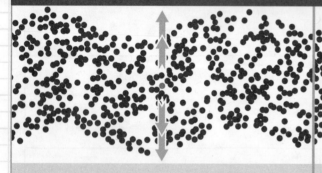

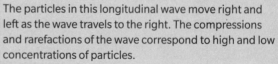

The particles in this transverse wave move up and down as the wave travels to the right. The crests and troughs of the wave are the high and low points in the wave.

The particles in this longitudinal wave move right and left as the wave travels to the right. The compressions and rarefactions of the wave correspond to high and low concentrations of particles.

7. Which statement best describes how the particles of a medium behave when a mechanical wave moves through the medium?

   A. Particles travel in the direction of the wave, away from the source of the wave.

   B. Particles travel in the direction that is perpendicular to the motion of the wave.

   C. Particles move as the wave passes them but do not move along with the wave.

   D. Particles stay in one place as the wave travels past them.

Sound, Media, and Wave Speed

The arrangement of and type of particles in a medium affect how the particles interact, and the particle interactions affect how waves travel through a medium. Recall that sound waves are a type of longitudinal mechanical wave and that sound waves can travel through gases, liquids, and solids. The speed of sound depends on the density of the medium through which the waves travel. The higher the density of the medium is, the faster sound travels in it. As a result, the speed of sound is lowest in gases and highest in solids. Changing the temperature of a medium may change the particle interactions, which would cause wave speed to vary in the same medium at different temperatures.

Medium	State	Speed (m/s)
Argon	gas	323
Air	gas	343
Neon	gas	435
Ethanol	liquid	1,162
Mercury	liquid	1,450
Water	liquid	1,482
Silver	solid	3,650
Steel	solid	5,200
Aluminum	solid	6,420

 8. **Do the Math** Use the table to calculate the average speed of sound in a gas, a liquid, and a solid, to the nearest m/s. Which of the following statements are true? Select all that apply.

A. The average speed of sound in a liquid is about 3.7 times the average speed of sound in a gas.

B. The average speed of sound in a solid is about 3.7 times the average speed of sound in a liquid.

C. The average speed of sound in a solid is about 0.07 times the average speed of sound in a gas.

D. The average speed of sound in a solid is about 13.9 times the average speed of sound in a gas.

Analyze How a Vacuum Affects Sound Waves

9. Think about how sound travels and decide whether a person outside the boxes would be able to hear the balloon pop. Explain why or why not.

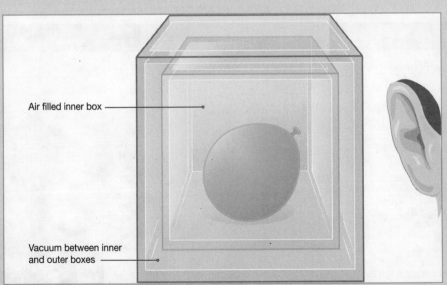

The space between the boxes is a vacuum.

Air filled inner box

Vacuum between inner and outer boxes

Analyzing How Waves Interact with a Medium

Wave Energy and Amplitude

If two waves have identical characteristics, except for their amplitude, the wave that has the greater amplitude carries more energy. Think about what happens to this energy as a wave travels through a medium away from its source.

Large earthquakes can occur as tectonic plates suddenly shift. In the area around this tectonic movement, the waves moving through the ground can be very destructive.

Farther away from the place where the initial disturbance occurred, the waves moving through the ground can still be felt, but are generally much less destructive.

10. Why do you think earthquakes are much more destructive closer to the initial disturbance than they are farther away?

Water Ripples

Ripples that move out from a disturbance in a pool of water are surface waves.

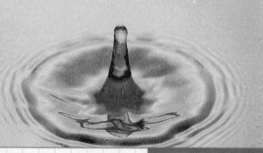

11. When the drop hits the water's surface, it generates a surface wave in the form of a ripple. What happens to the wave as it expands outward from the initial disturbance?

Explore Online

Mechanical Waves Spread Out

Mechanical waves spread out through a medium over time, and they spread out in as many directions as they are able. Surface waves on water spread out in a circle around the original disturbance, and sound waves in the air spread out as a sphere around the source of the sound. As a wave spreads out, energy is spread over a larger area. The area over which the energy spreads is related to the diameter of a sphere with the source at the center. As a result, the amplitude of a wave varies with diameter, as shown in the graph. One reason that distant sounds are quiet is that less energy reaches a listener who is farther away than one who is closer.

12. How does the energy of the wave in the graph change with the diameter of a sphere around the wave's source and why might this be occurring?

   A. The energy is decreasing because the amplitude of the wave is decreasing.

   B. The energy is not changing because the amplitude is constant.

   C. The energy is not changing because the frequency is constant.

   D. The energy is decreasing because the frequency of the wave is decreasing.

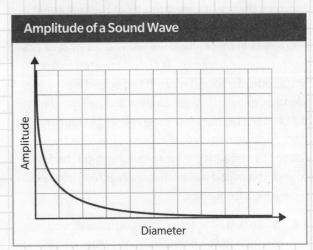

Absorption

Mechanical waves, such as sound waves, cause particles in a medium to move. As a wave passes through a medium, the medium's particles move and bump into one another, which transfers energy. During this movement, some of the wave's energy is converted into thermal energy by friction. **Absorption** is the conversion of a wave's energy into other forms of energy in the medium that the wave is traveling in. When energy is absorbed by a medium, the medium gains energy, and the wave loses that energy.

13. Dolphins locate objects underwater using high-frequency waves that can travel a few hundred meters. Whales communicate using low-frequency sounds that can travel hundreds of kilometers. Why do you think these sounds travel different distances?

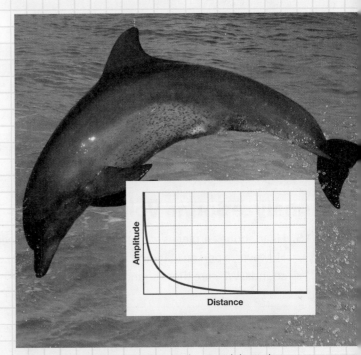

Dolphins and whales make sounds that travel through water. The graph shows how the amplitude of a sound wave changes as it moves farther from the source of the sound.

Absorption and Frequency

Absorption can vary based on the frequency of the wave. Generally, a high-frequency wave will lose more energy to absorption than a low-frequency wave will lose. The more a particle moves, the more energy it loses because of friction. High-frequency waves move a medium's particles more often. The higher the frequency of a wave is, the more energy it will lose to absorption and the more energy is converted into thermal energy. This conversion of energy into thermal energy is similar to what happens when you warm your hands using friction. Rubbing your hands against one another slowly will not generate much thermal energy, but when you rub your hands quickly, the friction between them will generate a lot of thermal energy.

All of the features of sound are related to the properties of mechanical waves. The volume, or how loud something sounds, is directly related to the amplitude of a sound wave. If two sound waves are identical except for their amplitude, the sound wave that has the higher amplitude will sound louder. Pitch, or how high or low a sound is, is directly related to frequency. If you hear a high-pitched sound, the sound waves that are reaching your ear have a high frequency.

14. When you hear sounds through a wall, you can hear lower-pitched sounds more clearly than higher-pitched sounds. Use a model to explain why this phenomenon occurs.

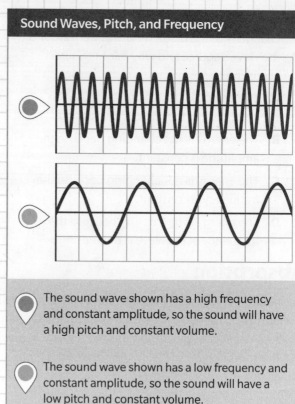

Sound Waves, Pitch, and Frequency

The sound wave shown has a high frequency and constant amplitude, so the sound will have a high pitch and constant volume.

The sound wave shown has a low frequency and constant amplitude, so the sound will have a low pitch and constant volume.

Analyze Sound Volume

15. Headphone earpieces can produce sounds that seem very loud to the listener. However, a person standing a meter away may not even be able to hear those same sounds. Why are these sounds so much quieter a short distance away?

_____

_____

_____

_____

Explaining the Behavior of Waves at Media Boundaries

Mechanical waves can travel through many different media, but they do not always move easily from one medium to another. Several things can occur when a wave reaches a new medium. For example, when you shout at a distant wall, you may hear an echo a few seconds later. An echo is an example of something that can occur when a mechanical wave contacts a new medium.

Echoes

Explore Online

16. When you yell in a gym and hear an echo, what might be happening to the sound wave?

Transmission

Consider what occurs when you hear sound through a wall. A sound wave traveled through the air, moved through the wall, and then traveled through air again to reach your ear. The sound wave crossed a boundary between two media twice before reaching your ear. A boundary is the surface or edge where two media meet. **Transmission** occurs when a wave travels through a boundary between media. On its path to your ear, the sound wave was first transmitted from the air into the wall. Then the sound wave traveled through the wall and encountered air as it emerged from the wall, and it was again transmitted to a new medium.

Energy absorbed by a medium is not transmitted. For example, loud music may sound faint when heard through a wall because the wall absorbs some of the sound and the person hears only the sound that transmits through the wall. Some waves are neither transmitted nor absorbed when they reach a boundary between media.

Reflection

When a wave encounters a new medium, it is not always transmitted into the new medium.

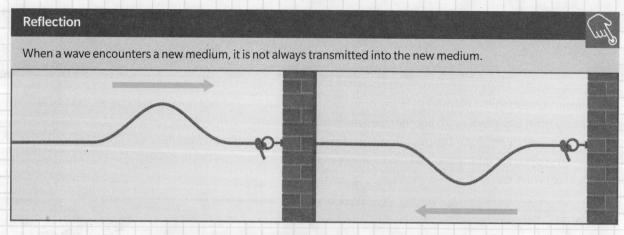

17. What occurs when the wave traveling through the rope encounters a new medium, the wall?

Reflection

When a wave encounters a boundary between two media, it does not always transmit into the new medium. Instead, the wave may bounce off the boundary and travel back through the original medium. When the wave bounces off the boundary, a **reflection** occurs. When you hear sound echo off a wall, you are hearing a reflected sound wave. The sound wave encountered a new medium, the wall, and was reflected.

Amplitude and Energy in Partial Reflection

The frequency of a wave does not change when it encounters a new medium, but the wavelength and amplitude may change.

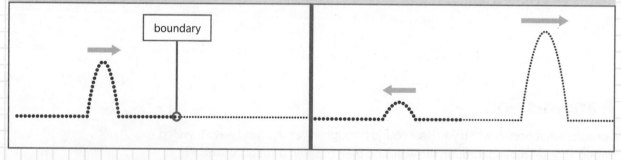

18. How would you best describe the behavior of the wave in the diagrams when it reaches the boundary between the big particles and the small particles?

19. What do you notice about the amplitude of the reflected wave?

Partial Transmission and Reflection

Generally, when a mechanical wave encounters a boundary between two different media, the wave is not entirely reflected or transmitted. Some of the wave can be transmitted into the new medium, and the remaining portion of the wave is reflected back into the original medium. This is why you can hear the sounds of a basketball game from outside a gym, even though there may be echoes inside the gym as well.

When a mechanical wave is partially reflected and partially transmitted, the original wave becomes two waves. The energy from the original wave is split between the transmitted wave and the reflected wave. Because the original wave's energy is split between the two new waves, each of the new waves will have less energy than the original wave had. Amplitude depends on the medium, so the transmitted and reflected waves' amplitudes could be very different.

Refraction

If you push a cart from a smooth floor to a carpeted floor, the carpet will cause the wheels to turn more slowly. If the right wheel hits the carpet first, the right wheel will turn more slowly than the left wheel will, causing the cart to turn to the right. This turning of a cart is an analogy for what happens to a wave when part of the wave changes speed.

The speed of a wave may change when it encounters a different medium. Part of the wave may speed up or slow down before another part of the wave, causing the wave to bend. When the path of a wave bends due to a change in wave speed, **refraction** occurs. The amount of refraction depends on the angle at which the wave encounters the boundary and how much the speed of the wave changes. Refraction can be observed in many types of waves, including seismic waves.

Note that when a wave crosses a boundary, its frequency always stays the same. Wave speed, frequency, and wavelength are related mathematically, so if the speed of a wave changes when it crosses a boundary, its wavelength must also change.

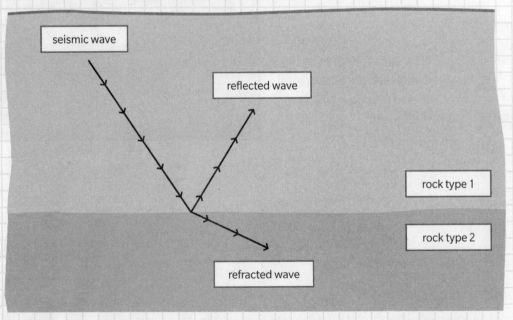

seismic wave

reflected wave

rock type 1

rock type 2

refracted wave

Seismic waves are partially reflected and transmitted at the boundary between different rock types. The transmitted waves refract because the waves travel at different speeds in the two media.

20. **Discuss** With a partner, discuss why a wave might bend when it changes speed. How might refraction look different if a wave speeds up compared to if it slows down when it moves into a new medium?

21. Draw The image shows a mechanical wave as it encounters a boundary between two media. Part of the wave may be reflected, but this is not shown. Draw what will happen to the part of the wave that passes into the new medium and slows down.

medium 1	medium 2

Engineer It
Explore Mechanical Waves in Medicine

Doctors use ultrasound, or high-frequency sound, to generate images of the inside of a person's body. Waves are sent through the body, bounce off organs, and then return to the imaging device. Ultrasound machines are often used instead of x-ray machines because scientific research has found that x-rays can damage living cells.

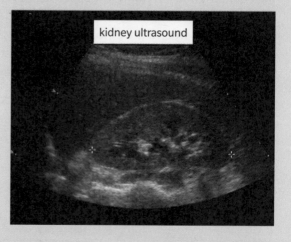

kidney ultrasound

22. What problem do ultrasound machines solve?

_____

_____

_____

_____

EVIDENCE NOTEBOOK

23. Ultrasounds use reflection and transmission to generate an image using sound waves. How might these same principles be used to visualize features and objects on the sea floor? Record your evidence.

© Houghton Mifflin Harcourt Publishing Company Image Credits: ©Zephyr/Science Source

Continue Your Exploration

Name: _____   Date: _____

Check out the path below or go online to choose one of the other paths shown.

| Designing Soundproof Rooms | • **People in Engineering**
• **Engineering to Prevent Earthquake Damage**
• **Hands-On Labs** 
• **Propose Your Own Path** | *Go online to choose one of these other paths.* |

When engineers design recording studios or practice spaces for musicians, they carefully consider ways to make the structures ideal for handling loud sounds. Engineers design the rooms to address several problems. For example, one problem is that echoes inside the room make hearing the desired sound difficult, and another problem is that some sounds are loud enough that they can be heard outside of the room. Engineers take into account the properties of different building materials and how the materials can be shaped and used to solve these problems.

1. Music practice spaces often have very thick walls made of dense materials such as cement. A sound wave moving through one of these walls moves a lot of particles and loses energy. What sound phenomenon are architects making use of with these walls? Explain your reasoning.

Continue Your Exploration

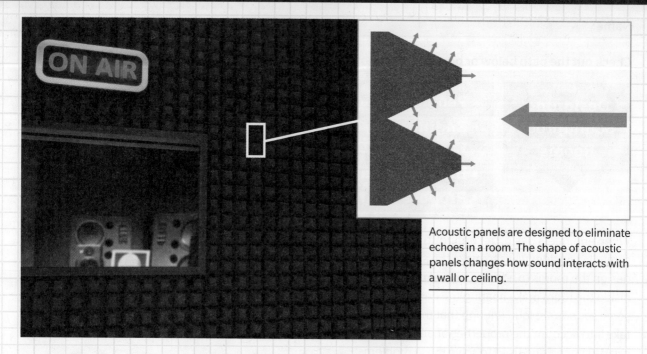

Acoustic panels are designed to eliminate echoes in a room. The shape of acoustic panels changes how sound interacts with a wall or ceiling.

2. Acoustic panels are designed to solve problems mainly related to the _____ of sound in a music studio.
   A. absorption
   B. reflection
   C. transmission

3. Compare the structure of the acoustic panels shown in the diagram to a flat wall and explain how the structure reduces echoes.

4. The recording booth shown has a window through which sound may be transmitted. Which of the following window structures would transmit the least amount of sound?
   A. a thin single pane of glass
   B. a thick single pane of glass
   C. double panes of glass with a dense gas between them
   D. double panes of glass with a vacuum between them

5. **Collaborate** With a partner, discuss ways in which the room you are currently in is or is not soundproofed. Consider ways that you could modify the room to better keep sound from escaping out of the room.

© Houghton Mifflin Harcourt Publishing Company • Image Credits: ©baldarik/Shutterstock

Can You Explain It?

Name: _____   Date: _____

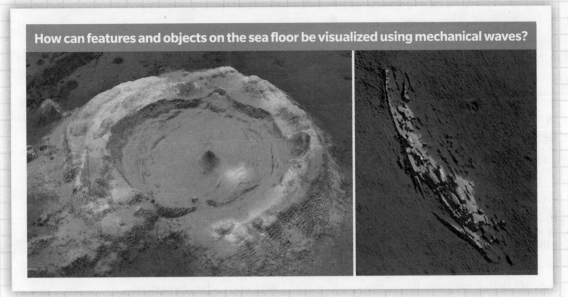

How can features and objects on the sea floor be visualized using mechanical waves?

EVIDENCE NOTEBOOK

Refer to the notes in your Evidence Notebook to help you construct an explanation of how features and objects on the sea floor can be visualized using mechanical waves.

1. State your claim. Make sure your claim fully explains how features and objects on the sea floor can be visualized using mechanical waves.

2. Summarize the evidence you have gathered to support your claim and explain your reasoning.

Checkpoints

Answer the following questions to check your understanding of the lesson.

Use the diagram to answer Question 3.

3. This diagram shows what happened after a wave traveling from the left encountered a boundary between its original medium and another, less dense medium. What happened at the boundary between media? Select all that apply.

   A. Some of the wave's energy was transmitted to the less dense medium.

   B. Part of the wave was reflected back into the original medium.

   C. Particles were carried from one medium to the other.

---

4. Sound is made up of transverse / longitudinal mechanical waves. As a sound wave travels through a medium, it permanently / temporarily moves particles in that medium. When the sound wave strikes a boundary between air and water, it will generally be completely / partially reflected.

Use the diagram to answer Question 5.

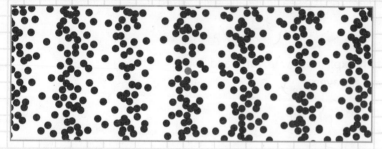

5. This diagram represents a sound wave traveling from left to right. As the wave passes the location of the particle represented by the red dot, how does the particle move?

   A. The particle travels from left to right along with the sound wave.

   B. The particle vibrates horizontally, moving both left and right.

   C. The particle vibrates vertically, moving both up and down.

---

6. As a sound wave spreads through the air, it moves the air particles smaller and smaller distances. What causes this change in the amplitude of the wave? Select all that apply.

   A. Amplitude decreases as the energy of a wave spreads across a greater amount of the medium.

   B. Amplitude decreases as medium's particles move away from the sound's source.

   C. Amplitude decreases as friction transforms energy from the sound wave.

Interactive Review

Complete this section to review the main concepts of the lesson.

Mechanical waves occur when energy moves through a medium due to the motion of particles.

A. When a mechanical wave travels through a medium, how does the wave affect the medium's particles?

As a mechanical wave travels through a medium, its amplitude can decrease due to the wave being spread across more matter and energy being transformed into other forms.

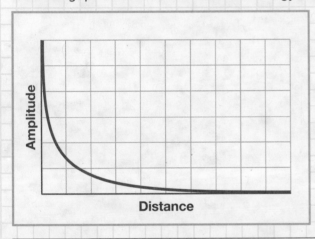

B. Describe why a sound wave's amplitude might decrease as it moves through a medium.

When a mechanical wave reaches a boundary between two media, the wave can be reflected, transmitted, or both. The transmitted wave may refract into the new medium.

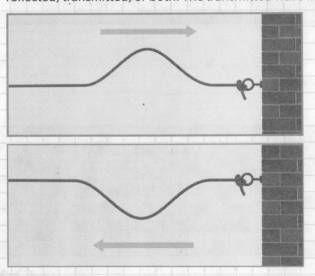

C. Describe how the properties of a wave may change as it is transmitted through a new medium.

Light Can Be Modeled as a Wave

© Houghton Mifflin Harcourt Publishing Company • Image Credits: ©Sven Robbe/EyeEm/Getty Images

Light streams into this space, and some areas are brightly lit while other areas remain in shadow.

Explore First

Observing Light Using a flashlight or another source of light, investigate how light behaves with one or more of the following devices: a kaleidoscope, a periscope, a mirror, or a prism. Why do you think light behaves the way it does with the devices?

Go online to view the digital version of the Hands-On Lab for this lesson and to download additional lab resources.

CAN YOU EXPLAIN IT?

Why does the same room lit with the same flashlight look different in these photos?

Observe what happens when the flashlight shines on the wall, the mirror, and the rug.

1. In each photo, the boy holds the same light source, a flashlight. Describe the appearance of the light in each photo. Note any similarities and differences.

 EVIDENCE NOTEBOOK As you explore the lesson, gather evidence to help explain how the behavior of light affects what we see and how we see it.

Exploring the Nature of Light

A light bulb, a burning log, and a candle are sources of light. Even living things, such as fireflies and some fish, can be sources of light. However, the most important source of light for life on Earth is the sun. Humans detect light using their eyes, and most people rely on their sense of sight in daily life. Think about how you interact with light on a daily basis. What other ways do you interact with light other than seeing with your eyes?

Light from the sun illuminates Earth.

2. Based on what you know about waves and light, do you think that light can be modeled as a wave? Explain why or why not.

The Speed of Light

Recall that mechanical waves, such as sound waves, require a medium through which to travel. Light, however, can travel through a vacuum. Light from the sun travels through space, which is a vacuum, to reach Earth. Light can also travel through different materials. Like mechanical waves, the speed of light varies in different media. Light travels most quickly through a vacuum, where it travels at a speed of about 300,000,000 m/s. Because this number is so large, it is often written using scientific notation as 3×10^8 m/s. Light tends to travel faster in lower-density media than in higher-density media. For example, light travels faster in air than it does in water.

3. **Do the Math** As light travels through a medium, it interacts with the particles of the medium and slows down. Use the graph to determine the ratios of the speeds of light in different media to one another and to the speed of light in a vacuum.

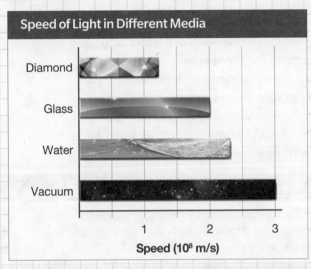

Speed of Light in Different Media

Diamond

Glass

Water

Vacuum

Speed (10^8 m/s)

The ratio of the speed of light through diamond to the speed of light through a vacuum is 5:12 / 3:4 / 12:5 . The ratio of the speed of light through glass to the speed of light through a vacuum is 2:3 / 3:4 / 3:2 . The ratio of the speed of light through diamond to the speed of light through glass is 1:2 / 5:8 / 8:5 .

Light and Energy

You may have noticed that when you leave an object in sunlight, the object gets warmer. Solar water heaters and solar ovens use this property of sunlight to heat water and cook food. Heating water or cooking food is otherwise a process that requires fuel to generate thermal energy. Solar panels use energy from sunlight to generate electrical energy.

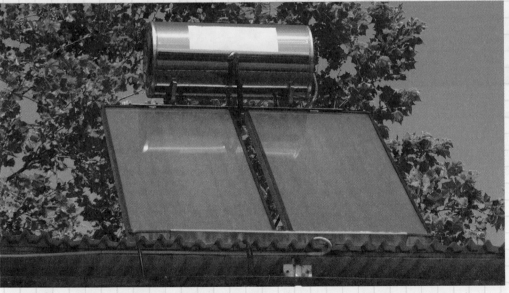

Solar water heaters are technology most commonly found in sunny climates. As water moves through the tubes of the heater, it is warmed by sunlight.

4. Waves transfer energy. When energy is absorbed / reflected /transmitted by matter, it transforms into thermal energy. The fact that sunlight can warm objects indicates that sunlight transfers energy, so it can / cannot be modeled as a wave.

The Electromagnetic Spectrum

When you look around, you see things that reflect light into your eyes. Light that humans readily see is called visible light. If a bee were in the room, the bee would see things differently than you do because bees can see a kind of light—called ultraviolet light—that you cannot see. Both ultraviolet light and visible light are part of a larger range of waves known as the *electromagnetic (EM) spectrum*. The EM spectrum is composed of many different types of EM waves, including x-rays, radio waves, and microwaves. **Electromagnetic waves** are waves made of vibrating electric and magnetic fields. Some of the waves, such as gamma rays, have high frequencies and short wavelengths and are highly energetic. Compared to gamma rays and visible light waves, radio waves have low frequencies and long wavelengths and carry less energy.

The Atmosphere Blocks Some EM Radiation

The sun gives off some radiation in every part of the EM spectrum. The atmosphere absorbs most of the higher-energy radiation, such as x-rays and gamma rays, and they do not reach the ground. Radio waves, visible light, and some ultraviolet light waves do reach the ground.

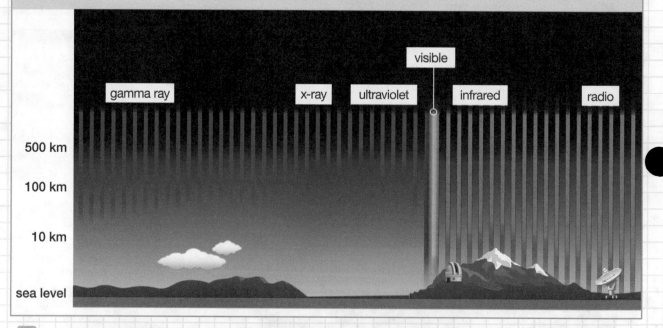

5. Language SmArts Waves that have longer wavelengths are absorbed more slowly by media than waves that have shorter wavelengths. Radio telescopes detect radio waves from space and can be used even on cloudy days. What advantages do radio telescopes on Earth have over visible light telescopes on Earth? Support your claim with evidence, and explain your reasoning.

Energy and Frequency

The energy of an electromagnetic wave depends on the wave's frequency. High-frequency, short-wavelength EM waves have more energy than low-frequency, long-wavelength EM waves have. The more energy EM waves have, the more dangerous they can be to living tissue. For example, x-rays have very high frequencies and carry a lot of energy. When working with x-rays, people must take special precautions, such as wearing a lead apron to block most of the x-rays. In contrast, radio waves, which have very low frequencies and carry less energy, are much safer. Radio waves are used often in consumer electronics such as radios, walkie-talkies, and baby monitors.

6. **Engineer It** When designing devices, engineers need to understand what makes some EM waves safe and others potentially dangerous. Engineers know that the safety of EM waves has to do with their frequency and the energy that they carry. A _higher_ / lower frequency means more energy and more energy means _more_ / less danger to human cells. Radio waves are _safe_ / not safe for humans because they are high-frequency / _low-frequency_ waves. Ultraviolet light waves, however, have _higher_ / lower frequencies, and they are not at all / _can be_ dangerous to human cells.

Compare Sound Waves and Light Waves

Electromagnetic waves behave similarly to mechanical waves in many ways, but they also have some differences. A vacuum is a space that has no particles of matter. Sound waves and light waves behave differently in a vacuum and in different media.

In this demonstration, tubing is connected to a pump that is removing air from the jar to produce a vacuum. As the air is removed, the buzzing timer sounds quieter and quieter.

7. Mechanical waves need a medium to travel; they cannot travel through a vacuum. Light _can_ / cannot travel through a vacuum; so light waves are / _are not_ mechanical waves. Sound waves _are_ / are not mechanical waves.

8. **Draw** Work with a partner to draw a model that explains the behavior of the sound waves and light waves when the air is completely removed from the container.

Modeling Light Waves

Throughout this lesson you have seen several different representations of light as waves. Think about some of the ways that waves are modeled. Different models help to explain the behavior of light in different situations.

Energy from the Sun

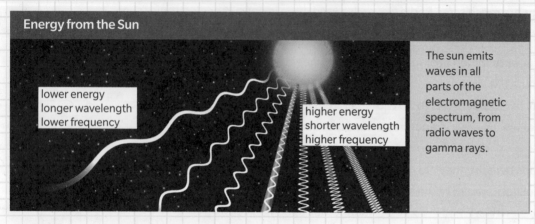

lower energy
longer wavelength
lower frequency

higher energy
shorter wavelength
higher frequency

The sun emits waves in all parts of the electromagnetic spectrum, from radio waves to gamma rays.

9. How is light represented in the diagram above?

Graphs of Light Waves

Graphs can be used to represent the wavelength and amplitude of light waves. Wavelength and amplitude correspond to the color and brightness of a light wave.

Wavelength, Amplitude, Color, and Brightness

Explore Online

Imagine a machine that lets you change the properties of visible light waves to see how they affect the color of light. Examine these images to see some possible results.

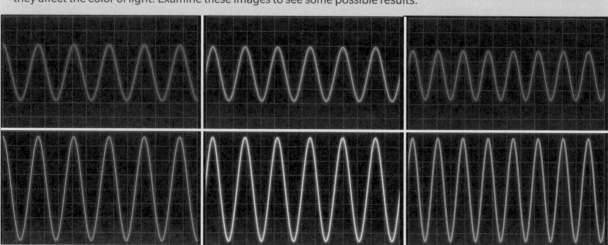

10. Do the Math The frequency, wavelength, and amplitude of a light wave can change. As the wavelength changes, so does the light's color / brightness . As the wavelength increases, frequency increases / decreases , which means that wavelength and frequency are directly / inversely proportional. Changing either of these properties changes / does not change the amplitude.

Ray Diagrams

When light travels through a medium that has constant properties, it travels in a straight line. The direction in which light travels can be represented using arrows called rays. Rays are commonly drawn so that they begin at the source of the light and point in the direction in which the light is moving. Because light travels in many different directions from a source, ray diagrams represent only one part of a situation, and the rays are drawn to model a specific behavior of a light wave. For example, when light encounters a boundary with a different medium, the light may change direction. This change in direction is shown by a ray pointing toward the boundary and a second ray pointing away from the boundary. Often the chosen ray points to the eye of an observer to demonstrate what the observer sees.

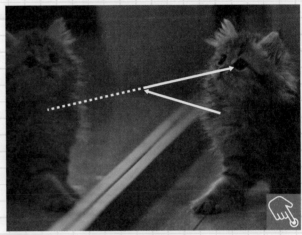

The ray changes direction because it hit a mirror.

11. Draw Sketch a ray diagram that shows how light from a light bulb helps you see a cat in a room.

Use Light Wave Models to Explain Operating Cost

An incandescent light bulb generates light by passing electrical energy through a thin wire called a filament. The filament converts this electrical energy into thermal energy and light energy. The *power* (energy per unit of time) that a light bulb uses is measured in watts. One watt (W) is equal to one joule per second. An incandescent bulb that uses more power is brighter than an incandescent bulb that uses less power. The bulbs generate light with the same wavelengths and frequencies.

12. Based on the information from the text and what you know about amplitude and brightness, draw two waves. One wave should represent a light wave from a red 30 W bulb, and the other should represent a wave from a red 60 W bulb.

13. Use frequency and amplitude to explain how your drawings model the two waves from the different light bulbs.

_____

_____

_____

_____

_____

_____

_____

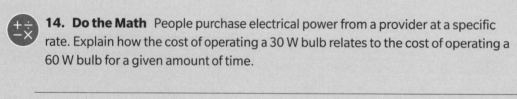 **14. Do the Math** People purchase electrical power from a provider at a specific rate. Explain how the cost of operating a 30 W bulb relates to the cost of operating a 60 W bulb for a given amount of time.

_____

_____

_____

_____

_____

Analyzing Human Perception of Light Waves

You analyzed mechanical waves such as sound waves and water waves and saw that, as the waves get farther from their source, they carry less energy. These energy losses occur because the waves spread out as they move away from the source, spreading their original energy over a greater area. Also, the medium through which the waves travel absorbs some energy, which transforms into other forms of energy and is lost from the wave. You know that the amount of energy carried by a wave is related to the amplitude of the wave. Think about how this behavior of mechanical waves can explain the behavior of light as it moves away from its source.

Brightness Versus Distance

Notice how light from a light source spreads as it moves farther from the source.

candlelight

car headlight

floodlight

15. **Draw** The graph shows how the brightness of car headlights changes as the light moves farther from the source. On this graph, sketch curves to show how the brightness of the light from a candle and from floodlights change with distance.

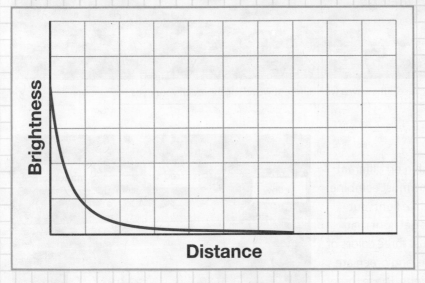

16. **Discuss** Together with a partner, analyze the photos and the graphs. Develop an explanation for why the relationship between brightness and distance is not linear and relate the brightness of the light to the energy of the light waves.

Light Waves and Color

Most waves in the electromagnetic spectrum are invisible to humans because their wavelengths are too short or too long for the human eye to see. However, electromagnetic waves in the visible range appear to humans as a spectrum of colors. Each color corresponds to a certain wavelength of light waves because the human brain interprets these different wavelengths as different colors. For example, blue light has a wavelength of about 475 nanometers, while red light has a wavelength of about 650 nanometers. When your eyes detect all wavelengths of visible light at once in equal proportions, you perceive white light. Sunlight contains all wavelengths of visible light so you see it as white light. Different wavelengths of light interact with matter in different ways, which is why specific colors are reflected when white light strikes an object.

You see many colors in these bubbles because light waves with different wavelengths reach your eyes.

Color Addition

Color addition is the process of combining different colors of light. You may think that you must combine all the colors of visible light to get white light, but that is not the only way. You can also get light that appears white by adding together just three colors of light: red, blue, and green. Red, blue, and green are referred to as the primary colors of light. These three colors of light can be combined in different ratios to produce many different colors. When two primary colors are added in equal amounts, secondary colors (yellow, magenta, and cyan) are formed.

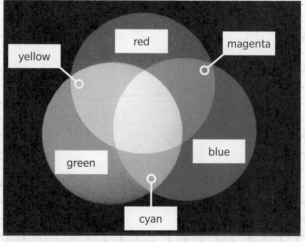

All three primary colors of light combine to produce white light. Red and green form yellow; red and blue form magenta; and blue and green form cyan.

© Houghton Mifflin Harcourt Publishing Company • Image Credits: (t) ©Rudi Sebastian/ Photolibrary/Getty Images; (b) ©Leonard Lessin/Science Source

17. When equal amounts of red, green, and blue light waves reach your eyes, the light appears red / green / blue / **white** / black because of a phenomenon called transmission / absorption / **color addition**.

Colors of Objects

Most objects do not generate and emit their own light, so why do these objects appear different colors? When light reaches an object, some of the light is reflected by the object, and some of the light is absorbed. The wavelengths of light that are reflected and reach your eyes determine what color you perceive an object to be.

Light Waves and the Perception of Color

The light rays in the image model various wavelengths of visible light. Compare how the incoming colors of light behave when they encounter the kitten's black fur, its white fur, and the green grass.

18. Draw In the space below, draw a model to illustrate why, in white light, an apple looks red and an orange looks orange.

Filters Affect Light Color

A filter is a medium that transmits certain wavelengths but absorbs others. For example, a red filter transmits the wavelengths corresponding to red light but blocks other visible light wavelengths. Look at the strawberry and the broccoli floret in the top photo. In white light, the strawberry appears mostly red and the broccoli appears mostly green.

If you put a red filter over the light source, as shown in the second photo, the strawberry still appears mostly red, but the broccoli appears mostly black because all colors except red were filtered out. The broccoli normally reflects green light and absorbs red light, but there is no green light to reflect, so the broccoli appears black.

If you replace the red filter with a green filter, your perception changes again. The strawberry now appears mostly black while the broccoli appears mostly green, as shown in the third photo.

19. Draw In white light, a banana appears yellow because it reflects both red and green wavelengths. Would it still appear yellow if you observed it through a blue filter? Draw a diagram to show the effect of a blue filter on your perception of the color of a banana.

Light Color Affects Our Perception of Objects

Explore how filtered light that strikes an object affects the perceived color of the object.

EVIDENCE NOTEBOOK

20. In what ways might an object or surface change the appearance of white light? Record your evidence.

Relate a Wave Model of Light to Brightness

21. As light moves farther from its source, it becomes less bright. How does a wave model of light explain the change in brightness? Select all that apply.

A. light spreads as it moves away from a source

B. light reflects off boundaries between media

C. energy is absorbed as it travels through different media

D. the amount of energy in an area decreases as light moves away from a source

Exploring Interactions of Light and Matter

Interactions between light and matter produce many common but spectacular effects, such as rainbows and optical illusions. Light, like other electromagnetic waves, can travel through empty space, but when light encounters a material, it can interact with the material in several ways. These interactions play an important role in how people see light.

The sky appears on the surface of a puddle on the ground.

22. What do you observe in the photo? Why do you think light behaves in this way?

Matter Can Reflect Light

You can see an object only when light from that object enters your eyes. Some objects, such as a flame, give off, or emit, their own light. Most objects do not emit light, but you can see those objects because light from another source bounces off them. The bouncing of light off a surface is called reflection. You can see the ground around the puddle in the photo, because sunlight reflected off the ground and entered your eyes.

Mirrors

A mirror has a very smooth surface that reflects light. Because mirrors are very smooth, they reflect light in a uniform way that results in an image when the reflected light enters your eyes. Other smooth surfaces, such as the surface of the water in the puddle in the photo, also reflect light in a uniform way and can also produce an image.

Light can reflect from surface to surface before it enters your eyes. Light from a lamp, for example, might have reflected off your skin, then reflected off the mirror, and then entered your eyes. When you look at the mirror, you see yourself!

Matter Can Transmit Light

How do the wrapped sandwiches in the photos differ? Why can you not see all three sandwiches beneath the wrappers equally well? The reason is how light interacts with matter. Different amounts of light pass through the different wrappers.

Light and other electromagnetic waves travel from a source in all directions, and they can travel through empty space or through matter. The passing of light waves through matter is called transmission. The medium through which light passes can transmit all, some, or none of the light. As you can see in the photos, the clear plastic wrap transmits almost all of the light, so you can clearly see the sandwich inside. When light travels through the waxed paper, only some of the light is transmitted. That sandwich is visible, but it looks fuzzy. The brown paper transmits none of the light, and as a result, you cannot see the sandwich within it at all.

Transmission and Absorption of Light

The clear plastic wrap around the first sandwich is an example of a transparent material. Light transmits through *transparent* materials, and objects can be seen clearly through them. Clean air, clean water, and smooth glass are also transparent. *Translucent* materials transmit light, but the light is scattered into many different directions. An object appears distorted or fuzzy through a translucent material. Frosted glass, tissue paper, and the waxed paper around the second sandwich are all examples of translucent materials.

These sandwiches are wrapped in clear plastic wrap, waxed paper, and brown paper. How do the different wrappers affect what you see?

Opaque materials do not let any light pass through them. Instead, they reflect light, absorb light, or both. When light enters a material but does not leave it, the light is absorbed. Absorption is the transfer of light energy to matter. Many materials, including wood, brick, and the brown paper around the third sandwich, are opaque.

23. Fill in the blanks to make the statements true.

   A. The sandwich wrapped in _____ is easy to see because the medium allows _____ of the light to pass through.

   B. The sandwich wrapped in _____ is obscured because the medium allows _____ of the light to pass through.

   C. The sandwich wrapped in _____ is not visible. That means the medium allows _____ of the light to pass through.

EVIDENCE NOTEBOOK

24. Think about the ways that matter interacts with light. How do these interactions relate to the flashlight images at the beginning of the lesson? Record your evidence.

© Houghton Mifflin Harcourt Publishing Company • Image Credits: ©Houghton Mifflin Harcourt

Hands-On Lab
Make a Penny Disappear

Observe how viewing an object through different media affects what you see.

MATERIALS
- beaker
- penny
- water

Procedure and Analysis

STEP 1 Place the penny on a flat surface like a lab table or a desk and carefully set the beaker on top of the penny.

STEP 2 Look at the penny from above the beaker and draw a ray diagram that models this situation.

STEP 3 Look at the penny through the side of the beaker and draw a ray diagram that models this situation.

STEP 4 Fill the beaker with water.

STEP 5 Look again at the penny from above the beaker and draw a ray diagram that models this situation.

STEP 6 Look at the penny again through the side of the beaker, from the same location as in Step 3. Draw a diagram to model this situation.

STEP 7 Use your ray diagrams to help explain why you are or are not able to see the penny in Steps 2, 3, 5, and 6.

© Houghton Mifflin Harcourt Publishing Company

Matter Can Refract Light

Light can travel through a vacuum or through a medium. When light of any wavelength travels through a vacuum, it always travels at the same speed. However, light travels slower in a medium. In fact, light of different wavelengths travels at different speeds in a medium. Shorter wavelengths are slowed more than longer wavelengths are. A prism is made of glass or another transparent material, and in a prism, the speed of shorter-wavelength violet light is less than the speed of longer-wavelength red light. These differences in speed cause the different wavelengths of light to separate.

Because light travels at different speeds through different media, the light waves bend when they hit the boundary between media at an angle. This bending of a light wave as it passes from one medium into another is called refraction. The amount and direction of the refraction depends on several factors, including the angle at which the light hits the boundary and the relative speed of light in the two media. Because different wavelengths of light travel at different speeds in a medium, each wavelength refracts at a different angle when white light hits a boundary between two media at an angle.

Light Traveling through a Prism

The top diagram shows that light is refracted when it enters and exits a prism. The bottom photo shows the result of the refraction. Note that the light beam on the bottom left is a reflected beam.

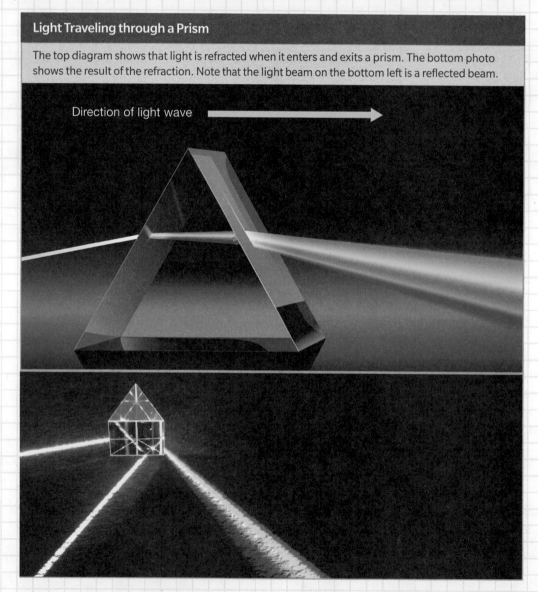

Direction of light wave

25. **Act** With a small group, act out what can happen when light encounters a new medium.

© Houghton Mifflin Harcourt Publishing Company • Image Credits: ©David Parker/Science Source

Optical Illusions Caused by Refraction

Your mind can play tricks on you because of refraction. The straw in the photo and the coin in the lab are two examples of optical illusions caused by refraction. When you look at an object that is underwater, the light reflecting off the object does not travel in a straight line. Because your brain always interprets light as traveling in a straight line, the images that you perceive do not match reality. For example, the light reflected by the upper part of the straw does, indeed, travel in the air in a straight line to your eye. But the light from the lower part of the straw is refracted as it passes from the water to the glass and refracted again when it passes into the air. The refracted light then travels in a straight line to your eye. Your brain interprets these light rays as coming from different sources, which causes the illusion that the part of the straw in the water is disconnected from the part out of the water.

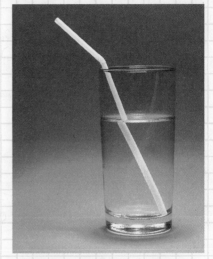

Refraction explains why the straw appears broken.

Refraction and Media

How much a light wave refracts at the boundary between two media depends on the media, the wavelength of the light, and the angle at which the light hits the boundary.

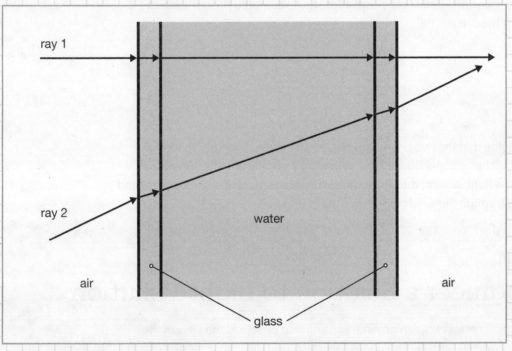

Ray 1 hits the initial boundary, and all other boundaries, at a 90° angle, and it does not refract. On the other hand, Ray 2 is refracted at a different angle at each boundary.

 26. Do the Math The ratio of the speed of light in air to the speed of light in glass is about 1.5. The ratio of the speed of light in water to the speed of light in glass is about 1.14. Explain whether you expect light to refract more when moving from air to glass or from water to glass.

Refraction and Prisms

The shape, material, and size of a prism affect how separated light waves passing through the prism will be. Look at the diagram to see how a prism can also be used to recombine separated light waves.

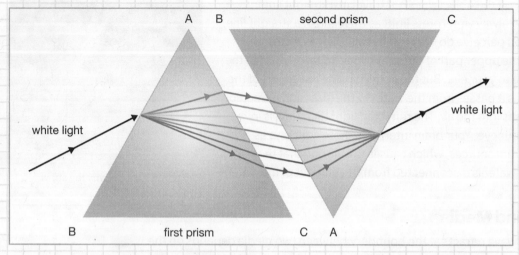

27. Notice how the light waves separate when they hit the first surface of the first prism. How does the shape and size of the prism affect how separated the light waves are when they exit the prism?

28. **Discuss** Imagine that the two prisms are moved and joined together to form a single block that has parallel sides. Think about this example and discuss with a partner why the light passing through a window appears much the same before and after it passes through the window.

Engineer It

Engineer a Solution to Light Pollution

Light pollution is the term for excess nighttime lighting that obscures the view of the night sky, negatively affects wildlife, and wastes energy.

29. **Draw** Outdoor lights are one contributor to light pollution. Apply your knowledge of the behavior of light waves to design a parking lot light that reduces excess nighttime light. Use ray diagrams to support your design.

Continue Your Exploration

Name: _____   Date: _____

Check out the path below or go online to choose one of the other paths shown.

What Color Should the Doghouse Be?

- **What Causes a Rainbow?**
- **Hands-On Labs** ✋
- **Propose Your Own Path**

Go online to choose one of these other paths.

Light energy that is not reflected by an object is absorbed or transmitted. When light energy is absorbed, it is converted into thermal energy. Combine this information with what you have learned about perceived color to determine which color to paint certain doghouses.

1. What are the needs of a doghouse in a warmer climate? What are the needs of a doghouse in a cooler climate?

2. How might color affect the warmth of a doghouse?

Continue Your Exploration

Light Reflectance Value (LRV) is a measurement that tells you how much light a color reflects. From that value, you can infer how much light the color absorbs. Designers and painters often use LRV in their work. The following table shows the LRV of the paint colors available to paint doghouses.

3. How does LRV of a color relate to the amount of light that the color absorbs? Explain.

Available Paint Colors		
Perceived color	Name of color	LRV
	Rosebud	62.26
	Crimson	12.35
	Sky	62.66
	Midnight	4.51
	Mint	74.93
	Forest	8.79

4. Which colors would you recommend for doghouses built in warmer climates? Use what you know about light and LRV to support your recommendation.

5. Which colors would you recommend for doghouses built in cooler climates? Use what you know about light and LRV to support your recommendation.

6. **Collaborate** In a small group, list at least eight common car colors and then use a Venn diagram to sort the colors by "good in hot weather" and "good in cold weather." The colors that overlap are good for both hot weather and cold weather. Support your claim and share your results with the class.

Can You Explain It?

Name: _____   **Date:** _____

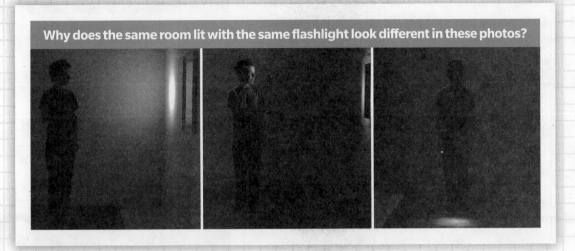

Why does the same room lit with the same flashlight look different in these photos?

EVIDENCE NOTEBOOK
Refer to the notes in your Evidence Notebook to help you construct an explanation for how a room lit with the same flashlight can look different.

1. State your claim. Make sure your claim explains how the same light source in the same room can produce such different results.

2. Summarize the evidence you have gathered to support your claim and explain your reasoning.

Checkpoints

Answer the following questions to check your understanding of the lesson.

Use the graph to answer Question 3.

3. Which statements are supported by the information in the graph? Select all that apply.

   A. Light travels at the same speed in water, glass, and diamond.

   B. Light travels the fastest in a vacuum compared to the various media.

   C. Light cannot travel through any media at all.

   D. Light travels slower in media than it does in a vacuum.

   E. Light can travel with or without a medium.

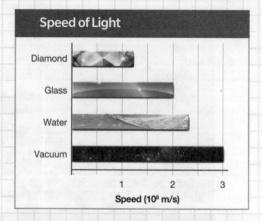

Speed of Light

Diamond
Glass
Water
Vacuum

Speed (10^8 m/s)

Use the photo to answer Questions 4–5.

4. What behavior of light is shown by the sphere?

   A. refraction

   B. absorption

   C. transmission

   D. reflection

5. Light travels in a straight / curved path. The image on the sphere appears curved because the sphere is a prism / mirror. As light hits the sphere's curved surface, light bounces off / bends around it at different angles, causing the image to appear distorted.

6. Some golfers use a blue filter to help see where their ball is in tall grass. The white golf ball will appear white / black / blue when viewed through the filter. Green grass around the ball will appear mostly white / black / blue / red when viewed through the filter, which makes seeing the ball easier.

7. A light wave travels through air toward water. Which statement describes the refraction of the light ray?

   A. The light stops traveling when it reaches the water.

   B. The light's energy transforms into thermal energy.

   C. The light changes direction when it reaches the water.

   D. The light bounces off the water and travels through the air.

8. The brightness of light is related to the light wave's wavelength / amplitude. The color of light is related to the light wave's wavelength / amplitude. Changing the amplitude of a light wave will / will not change its wavelength.

© Houghton Mifflin Harcourt Publishing Company • Image Credits: ©Robert Lachman/Getty Images

Interactive Review

Complete this section to review the main concepts of the lesson.

Light is part of the electromagnetic spectrum. Light transfers energy and can travel through a vacuum.

A. Which behavior of light indicates that light transfers energy? Explain your reasoning.

Modeling light as a wave helps to explain the behavior of light in different situations.

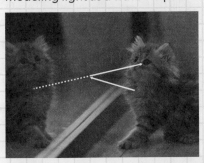

B. Explain why having different models of light waves is useful.

The amplitude and wavelength of a light wave affect the perceived brightness and color of light.

C. Use a wave model of light to explain why white light can be separated to show different colors.

At the boundary between media, light may be reflected, transmitted, refracted, or absorbed.

D. What types of interactions between light and matter can change the direction that light travels?

Energy from Sunlight Causes Earth's Seasons

Fall leaves change color as weather cools and leaves are no longer able to produce food for the tree. This photo of Virginia's Sherando Lake shows an example of this phenomenon.

Explore First

Exploring Solar Heating Place two identical pieces of dark construction paper outside: put one in sunlight and one in shade. After several minutes, touch the pieces of paper and compare their temperatures. What do you observe? With a partner, discuss possible explanations for your observations.

CAN YOU EXPLAIN IT?

Why is winter colder than summer?

This photo shows a cold day in the Tatra Mountains in Zakopane, Poland. Even though the sun is shining, the temperature is cold enough that snow stays on the ground.

Explore Online

1. Look at the photo, which was taken in the middle of the day. What season do you think it is? What evidence do you see to support your answer?

2. One day is defined as an amount of time equal to 24 hours. Why do you think people say winter days are shorter than summer days?

 EVIDENCE NOTEBOOK As you explore the lesson, gather evidence to help explain why winter days are colder than summer days are.

Analyzing Energy from the Sun in the Earth System

Waves from the Sun

The sun emits energy in all directions in the form of electromagnetic waves. When these waves reach Earth, they interact with the atmosphere and Earth's surface in a variety of ways.

3. Think about moving from an area in direct sunlight to an area in the shade. What differences do you notice in the way you feel in these two situations?

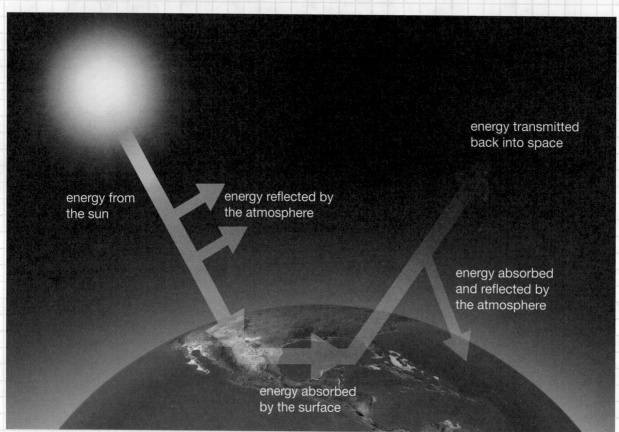

The energy from the sun warms the atmosphere and Earth's surface.

4. When waves from the sun reach Earth's atmosphere, the waves behave in different ways depending on their wavelength. Some of the waves are reflected off / refracted by / transmitted through the atmosphere back into space. Some of the waves are absorbed by / transmitted through the atmosphere and reach Earth's surface. Some of the waves are absorbed by the atmosphere and never reach Earth's surface. When waves are reflected / refracted / transmitted / absorbed, the energy transforms into thermal energy.

Seasons of the Year

A **season** is a division of the year that is associated with particular weather patterns and daylight hours. Weather conditions and daily temperatures at any location on Earth follow a predictable cycle throughout the year. During a year, many places on Earth experience four seasons. Winter may be cold and may bring snow and ice. Spring occurs as winter changes to summer, and the temperatures in the area increase.Summer may be hot. Fall, or autumn, occurs as temperatures decrease and winter returns. The farther from the equator you go, the greater the differences in the seasons. For example, winter and summer at a location near the equator may be very similar to each other.

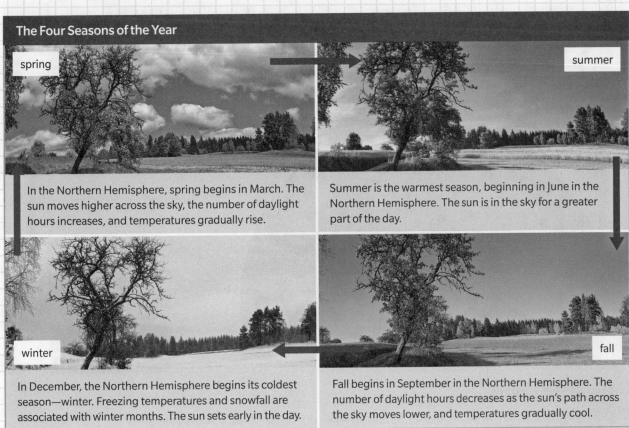

The Four Seasons of the Year

spring

In the Northern Hemisphere, spring begins in March. The sun moves higher across the sky, the number of daylight hours increases, and temperatures gradually rise.

summer

Summer is the warmest season, beginning in June in the Northern Hemisphere. The sun is in the sky for a greater part of the day.

winter

In December, the Northern Hemisphere begins its coldest season—winter. Freezing temperatures and snowfall are associated with winter months. The sun sets early in the day.

fall

Fall begins in September in the Northern Hemisphere. The number of daylight hours decreases as the sun's path across the sky moves lower, and temperatures gradually cool.

5. Draw Make a diagram that shows the seasonal differences where you live.

Changes across the Seasons

Because of Earth's rotation, you see the sun appear to move across the sky. For people living on the equator, the path of the sun in the sky does not change very much throughout the year. The sun rises on the eastern horizon, goes nearly overhead, and then sets on the western horizon. The sun reaches its highest point in the sky at about noon. Daytime lasts about 12 hours all year long, and the weather is nearly always warm. But as you move north or south away from the equator, the sun's path in the sky changes during the year. For example, in the Northern Hemisphere, the sun rises north of east in the summer and rises south of east in the winter. Sunsets follow a similar pattern. Summer sunsets in the Northern Hemisphere are north of west, while winter sunsets are south of west. As a result, the sun's path changes as seasons change.

The Path of the Sun in Summer and Winter in the Northern Hemisphere

6. Write summer or winter to label each path of the sun.

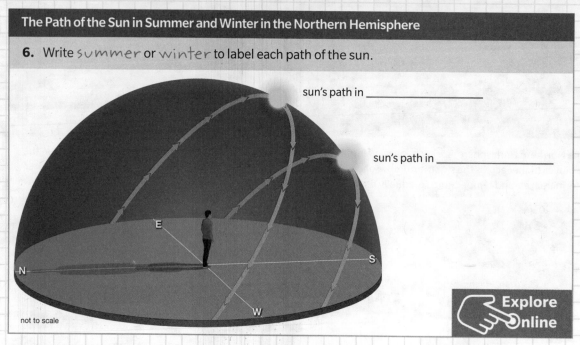

sun's path in _____

sun's path in _____

not to scale

Explore Online

Daylight Hours

During winter, it may be dark outside when you wake up for school and dark again soon after school ends. The sun does not go very high in the sky so its path across the sky is shorter. Because the sun is not up in the sky very long, there is less daylight time during this time of year. As a result, there is less time for sunlight to warm Earth during the daytime and more time for Earth to cool during the longer nighttime hours. The shortest amount of daylight time occurs on December 21 or 22 in the Northern Hemisphere.

During summer, the sun goes higher in the sky and days are longer because more time is needed for the sun to complete its longer path across the sky. Summer is warmer than winter because the sun is up for a longer period of time. There are more hours of daylight to warm Earth during the daytime, and fewer nighttime hours for Earth to cool. The day that has the greatest amount of daylight time is June 20, 21, or 22 in the Northern Hemisphere.

EVIDENCE NOTEBOOK

7. Use the path of the sun across the sky to help to explain why winter has shorter days than summer has. Record your evidence.

© Houghton Mifflin Harcourt Publishing Company

Hands-On Lab
Model Sunlight Distribution

Do the Math Explore what happens when light is spread out compared to when it is not spread out.

Procedure

STEP 1 Work with a partner. One partner shines a flashlight straight down on graph paper from a height of 15 cm. Using a protractor, the second partner makes sure the light strikes the paper at a 90° angle. The second partner then traces around the lit area on the paper with a pencil and labels it *90°*.

STEP 2 Switch holding the flashlight between partners. Keep the flashlight at the same height as it was in Step 1 (15 cm). Using the protractor, one partner guides the other to change the position of the flashlight so that the angle of the light striking the paper is 60°. That partner traces the lit area and labels it *60°*.

STEP 3 Next, using the protractor, change the angle so that the light striking the paper is 30°. Trace the lit area and label it *30°*.

STEP 4 Calculate the total area of each lit area using the following method:

   a. Count and record the number of full squares in each area.
      Example: 4 full squares

   b. Count the number of partial squares and divide the number by 2.
      Example: 12 partial squares ÷ 2 = 6

   c. Add the number of full squares to the number calculated for partial squares to find the total area. Example: 4 + 6 = 10

Angle of light	4a. Full squares	4b. Partial squares	4c. Total area
90°			
60°			
30°			

Analysis

STEP 5 Describe the relationship between the angle of light and area lit. How might this relate to sunlight distribution?

Energy from the Sun

There are two reasons why a place on Earth receives different amounts of the sun's energy in summer and winter: changes in the length of the sun's path across the sky and changes in the height of the sun at midday. In the summer, the sun has a longer path across the sky, which means the sun is in the sky for a longer period of time. There are more hours of daylight, so there is more time for Earth to absorb solar energy, and fewer hours of darkness for Earth to cool before the next day.

The height of the sun in the sky determines the angle at which the sunlight strikes Earth. As demonstrated in the activity, when the sun is overhead, the light is less spread out and the energy on each square meter is more intense. The amount of energy striking a small area will result in warmer temperatures than the same amount of energy striking a spread-out area. In summer, when the sun is higher in the sky, solar energy is more concentrated, but in winter, when the sun is lower in the sky, the sun's energy reaches Earth at a lesser angle. The angle at which sunlight strikes Earth influences Earth's temperatures, making it warmer in summer and colder in winter.

In addition to changing the distribution of sunlight over Earth's surface, the height affects the intensity of the energy at Earth's surface. As the electromagnetic waves from the sun pass through the atmosphere, energy is absorbed. Solar energy passes through more atmosphere when it strikes Earth at a lesser angle, making the sun's rays striking Earth less intense.

As the sun moves lower in the sky, the energy from sunlight is spread over a larger and larger area. A given amount of ground gets all of the light when the sun is directly overhead but gets only a part of the light when the sun strikes at an angle.

8. **Discuss** Together with a partner, talk about the amount of solar energy that falls on a given area. What happens when light is not spread out, and what happens when the light is more spread out? Relate this idea to the sun's energy and Earth.

 9. **Language SmArts** On a separate sheet of paper, write a short essay to compare what you observed in your investigation to what you saw in the image and what you read about the angles of sunlight striking Earth.

Patterns of Sunlight and Latitude

Electromagnetic waves from the sun are often referred to as sunlight. The rays of sunlight move in straight lines, and because the sun is so far away, the rays that strike Earth are very nearly parallel. Because of Earth's spherical shape, these parallel rays strike Earth most directly near the equator. As you move from the equator to the poles, the rays strike at lesser angles.

The diagram shows Earth lit by the sun on a day in the spring or fall. The diagram shows that the sun appears overhead as viewed from the equator, which means that people who live on or near the equator feel the intense energy of the sun. On the other hand, people who live at the North Pole or the South Pole would see the sun on this same day as very low in the sky. This diagram helps to illustrate why it is nearly always warm near the equator and cold at the poles.

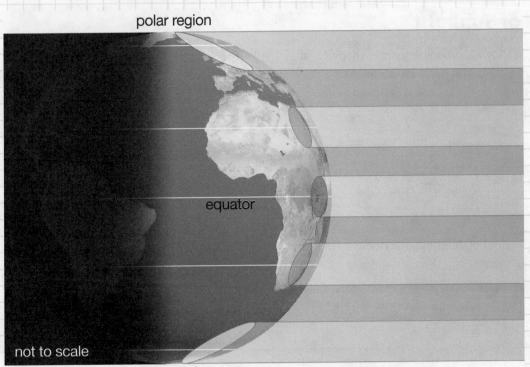

polar region

equator

not to scale

polar region

Due to the shape of Earth, sunlight strikes different latitudes on Earth's surface at different angles.

10. Imagine three people pointing toward the sun: a person at the equator, a person at the North Pole, and a person somewhere in between. Describe where in the sky each person is pointing.

11. Which of these statements describes the differences in sunlight striking Earth at different latitudes? Select all that apply.

 A. The intensity of the sun's energy received at the equator is greater than the intensity of the energy received at the poles.

 B. Sunlight strikes at a greater angle at the equator, which spreads out the sunlight.

 C. As you move away from the equator, the rays of sunlight striking Earth are no longer parallel.

 D. Sunlight passes through less atmosphere at the equator, so more sunlight gets through, which makes locations around the equator hotter.

Analyze How Earth's Shape Affects Patterns of Sunlight

12. The diagram shows an imaginary, cube-shaped planet. Explain how the range of temperatures at noon at different latitudes on a cube-shaped planet would compare to temperatures on the spherical Earth.

_____

_____

_____

_____

_____

13. Draw To the right of the cube, draw a model of the way the sun's rays would strike a cube-shaped planet.

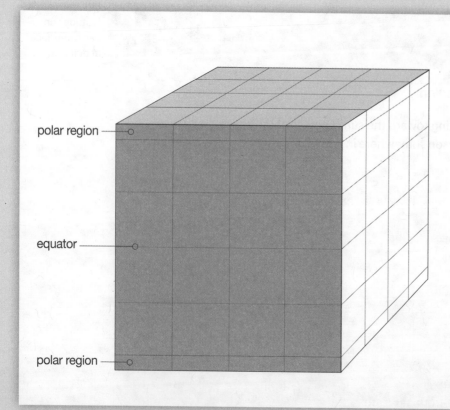

Analyzing an Earth-Sun Model to Explain Seasons

Earth orbits the sun in a predictable pattern. The pattern of Earth's seasons depends on how much sunlight reaches different areas of Earth as the planet moves around the sun. One complete orbit around the sun is called a revolution. One complete revolution takes one year.

Earth-Sun Models

Earth has a nearly circular, elliptical orbit around the sun. Earth also rotates around its north-south axis, which is an imaginary line passing through Earth from pole to pole.

14. What does the model in the first diagram show? Select all that apply.

    A. Every place on the planet gets 12 hours of light and 12 hours of dark each day.

    B. Temperature conditions on the planet change depending on distance from the sun.

    C. There are colder temperatures at the poles and warmer temperatures at the equator but no temperature changes during the year.

15. Does the first model explain the seasons that occur on Earth? Give at least one example to support your answer.

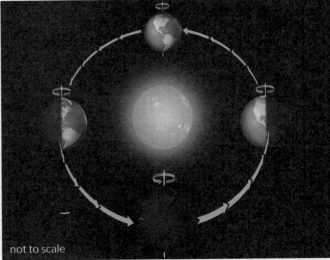

not to scale

Earth has a nearly circular orbit around the sun. This model of a fictional Earth shows an axis that is not tilted.

Unlike the planet in the first model, Earth's axis is not perpendicular to the plane of Earth's orbit around the sun. Earth's axis is tilted 23.5° from perpendicular to the plane of its orbit. This tilt remains the same throughout Earth's orbit, so Earth's axis is pointed in the same direction no matter where Earth is in its orbit around the sun.

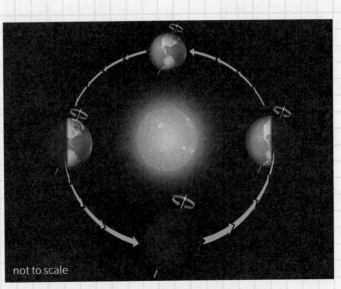

not to scale

This model shows Earth with its axis tilted 23.5°.

Hands-On Lab
Model Patterns of Sunlight throughout Earth's Revolution

Model the tilt of Earth in the Earth-sun system and show the way different areas of Earth receive more or less sunlight throughout the year.

Procedure

STEP 1 Use the modeling clay to make a base for your foam ball sphere.

STEP 2 With the marker, mark both poles and draw an equator on the sphere. Push the toothpick carefully through the sphere from pole to pole.

STEP 3 Insert the toothpick into the base and use the protractor to set the tilt of the axis at 23.5° from vertical.

STEP 4 Cut the construction paper so that it is a square and then fold it exactly in half. Draw a line along the fold. Use the protractor to mark 90° on both sides of the line and connect those marks. Label the four connected folds beginning with *Spring* and moving counterclockwise to label *Summer*, *Fall*, and *Winter*.

STEP 5 Place the light source on the center of the paper where the lines cross to act as the sun in the model.

STEP 6 Set the sphere directly on *Summer* with the North Pole (the top of the toothpick) tilting toward the light. Observe where the sphere is light and dark. Record your data by drawing and shading to show your *Summer* sphere in the table below.

STEP 7 **Keep the angle and direction that the sphere is pointing the same.** Move the sphere to *Fall*. Observe where the light falls and record your data in the table for *Fall*.

STEP 8 Repeat Step 7, moving the sphere to *Winter* and then *Spring*.

© Houghton Mifflin Harcourt Publishing Company

MATERIALS
- ball, foam, 1"
- clay, modeling non-drying
- light source
- marker
- paper, construction
- protractor
- ruler, metric
- toothpick

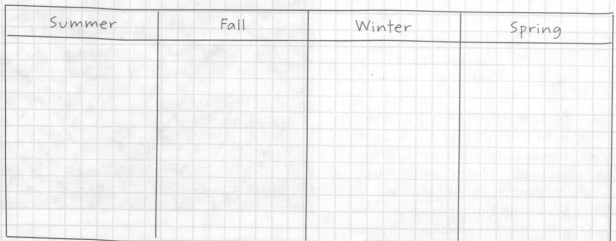

Summer	Fall	Winter	Spring

Analysis

STEP 9 What did you observe about sunlight on Earth in winter? Use your observations to explain why the Northern Hemisphere has lower temperatures in winter.

STEP 10 When the Northern Hemisphere tilts away from the sun, what season would you expect to experience in the Southern Hemisphere? Explain your answer.

The Tilt of Earth

The spherical shape of Earth explains why it gets colder as you get closer to the poles and why the height of the sun appears lower in the sky as you get closer to the poles. But these ideas alone do not completely explain why it is warmer in summer than in winter.

What did you learn as your model Earth moved around the model sun? Because Earth's tilt did not change, the amount of sunlight reaching a specific area of Earth did change. As Earth orbits the sun, the area of Earth that is pointed more toward the sun changes because Earth is always tilted in the same direction. So, the reason that Earth has seasons is because of a combination of Earth's tilt and Earth's revolution.

When the Northern Hemisphere points toward the sun, the Southern Hemisphere points away from the sun. As a result, seasons in the Southern Hemisphere are opposite from those in the Northern Hemisphere. In December, it is winter in Canada and summer in Australia.

16. Do the North Pole and the South Pole always stay in the same position relative to the sun? Explain your reasoning.

© Houghton Mifflin Harcourt Publishing Company

Earth's Revolution around the Sun

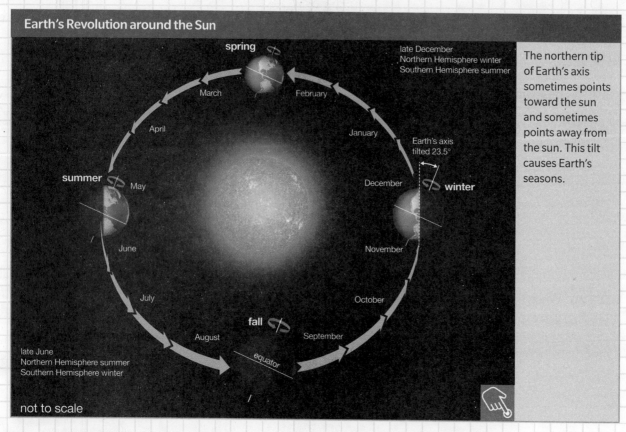

spring

March

April

summer

May

June

July

August

fall

equator

September

October

November

December

winter

January

February

late December
Northern Hemisphere winter
Southern Hemisphere summer

Earth's axis
tilted 23.5°

late June
Northern Hemisphere summer
Southern Hemisphere winter

not to scale

The northern tip of Earth's axis sometimes points toward the sun and sometimes points away from the sun. This tilt causes Earth's seasons.

17. It is summer in the hemisphere tilted *away from / toward* the sun, and it is winter in the hemisphere tilted *away from / toward* the sun. The seasons are *the same / reversed* in the Northern and Southern Hemispheres.

The Effect of Earth's Tilt on Daylight Hours

The number of hours of daylight increases as spring changes to summer because of Earth's tilt. If Earth had no tilt, days and nights would last about 12 hours each day everywhere. Because of the tilt, areas pointed toward the sun have more hours of daylight than those areas pointed away from the sun have.

Hours of Daylight by Latitude

18. Complete the labels to show how much daylight an area at each latitude would have when Earth is in this position.

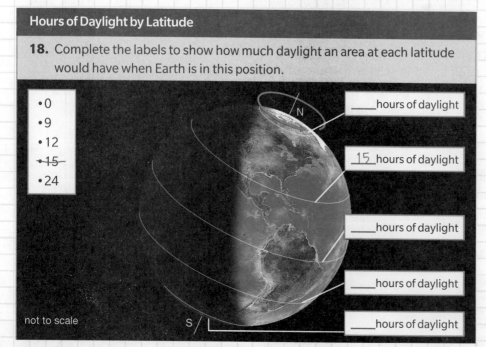

- •0
- •9
- •12
- •~~15~~
- •24

N

_____ hours of daylight

_15_ hours of daylight

_____ hours of daylight

_____ hours of daylight

S

_____ hours of daylight

not to scale

The Solstices and Equinoxes

Solstices mark the two days of the year when Earth's axis is tilted directly toward or away from the sun. The June solstice, also called the summer solstice, occurs when Earth's north axis is tilted toward the sun, between June 20 and June 22. The June solstice is the day of the year that has the greatest number of daylight hours in the Northern Hemisphere. This longest day of the year in the Northern Hemisphere is at the same time as the shortest day of the year in the Southern Hemisphere.

The December solstice, also called the winter solstice, occurs when Earth's north axis is tilted away from the sun, around December 21. The December solstice is the day with the fewest number of daylight hours in the Northern Hemisphere. In the Southern Hemisphere, the December solstice is the longest day of the year.

The days that begin spring and fall are marked by the equinoxes. Earth's axis does not tilt directly toward or away from the sun. The word *equinox* means "equal night," and on an equinox, there are equal hours of day and night at all locations on Earth.

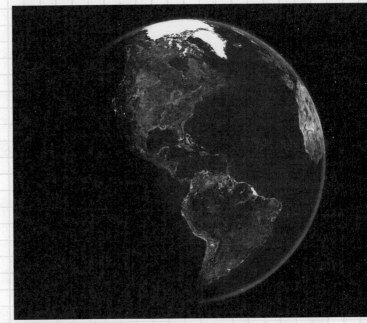

On the June solstice, there are 24 hours of daylight at the North Pole, 12 hours of daylight at the equator, and 24 hours of darkness at the South Pole.

19. The solstices / equinoxes mark the dates on which Earth's axis is tilted directly toward or away from the sun. The days get shorter / longer as you move from the June solstice to the December solstice in the Northern Hemisphere.

The Tilt of Earth Affects the Energy Received from the Sun

Earth's tilt affects the temperatures at different locations on Earth. Because of Earth's tilt, some parts of Earth receive more solar energy than others. At the North Pole, Earth's tilt means that the sun rises above the horizon in mid-March and continues to shine without completely setting until mid-September. But because the sun shines on the North Pole at a lesser angle instead of striking from directly overhead, less energy is received in a given area at the North Pole than at the equator. When sunlight strikes at a lesser angle, the light spreads out. So, although daylight lasts longer at the North Pole than at the equator, the temperature is not as warm.

The angle at which sunlight strikes a particular location on Earth changes as Earth revolves around the sun. Areas are warmer where sunlight is not as spread out, such as in those areas around the equator.

20. When the South Pole is tilted toward / away from the sun, the Southern Hemisphere experiences winter. The amount of the sun's energy that strikes the area increases / decreases as compared to the sun's energy in the summer. The daylight hours are longer / shorter, and the area temperatures increase / decrease.

Note that Earth's distance from the sun is not what determines the seasons. In fact, Earth is closest to the sun around January 3 and farthest from the sun around July 4. It is Earth's tilt that determines the seasons.

21. How can the tilt of Earth be used in an explanation of why winter has cold temperatures and short daylight hours? Record your evidence.

Relate Patterns of Sunlight and Solar Panels

Solar panels capture light from the sun and convert the solar energy into electrical energy. The more sunlight that reaches your solar panels, the more electrical energy you can generate.

How would you position solar panels to receive the maximum amount of light energy from the sun? You know that when the sun's energy is less spread out, the amount of energy reaching that location on Earth is greatest. One way to get maximum light energy to the solar panels is by changing the angle of the panels to directly face the sun. The angle at which the panels capture the most solar energy depends on how close to the equator the panels are located.

22. **Engineer It** An engineer must decide how to set up a field of solar panels. Which of these should the engineer consider to capture the maximum amount of solar energy? Select all that apply.

 A. how far away the location of the solar panel field is from the equator

 B. that the panels will be closer to the sun in the summer than in the winter

 C. whether the solar panels can be adjusted to a 90° angle to face the incoming light rays

 D. whether the panels should face north, south, east, or west

These solar panels are adjusted to the best angle at which to capture solar energy.

23. The photo of these solar panels was taken at noon. Explain whether you think these panels are in an area close to or far from the equator.

_____

_____

_____

_____

_____

Continue Your Exploration

Name: _____   Date: _____

Check out the path below or go online to choose one of the other paths shown.

> **Land of the Midnight Sun**

- **Exploring Ways Organisms Adjust to the Seasons**
- **Hands-On Labs** 🖐
- **Propose Your Own Path**

Go online to choose one of these other paths.

The *land of the midnight sun* describes parts of Earth where, for at least some of the year, a part of the sun is visible above the horizon for 24 hours of the day, including at midnight. Midnight sun occurs in the summer months in places north of the Arctic Circle and south of the Antarctic Circle.

Day and night at the poles are not at all like day and night on the rest of Earth. At the poles, there are six months of daylight and then six months of darkness in a year, which means that the poles experience one sunrise and one sunset each year.

Areas inside the Arctic and Antarctic Circles also experience periods during the year in which there is darkness or daylight for more than 24 hours. But as you move farther away from the poles these periods get shorter. Locations between the Arctic Circle and the equator and between the Antarctic Circle and the equator do not have days with a midnight sun.

Explore Online

During summer in the Arctic, the sun travels in a complete circle near the horizon but does not set. This time-lapse photo was taken at ten-minute intervals before and after midnight near Kópasker, Iceland.

1. If the sun is out all day, why is it not warm during an Arctic summer?

Continue Your Exploration

2. When people above the Arctic Circle are experiencing the midnight sun, what are people at the South Pole experiencing?

A. long nights with only a few hours of sunlight

B. equal hours of day and night

C. stars and 24-hour nights

D. 24-hour days and a midnight sun

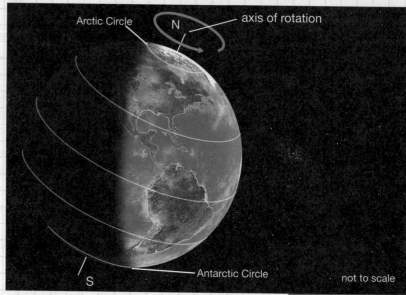

The midnight sun is due to the tilt of Earth's axis. This image shows Earth's orientation to the sun during summer in the Northern Hemisphere.

3. **Draw** Sketch a model of Earth similar to the one above, but instead show Earth when the areas near the South Pole are experiencing midnight sun. Indicate where sunlight falls and where it is dark. Label Earth's axis and indicate the area south of the Antarctic Circle.

4. **Collaborate** Work with a partner to make a poster that explains the midnight sun. Include some kind of labeled diagram on your poster.

Can You Explain It?

Name: _____ Date: _____

Why is winter colder than summer?

EVIDENCE NOTEBOOK

Refer to the notes in your Evidence Notebook to help you construct an explanation for why winter is colder than summer.

1. State your claim. Make sure your claim fully explains the differences between winter and summer.

2. Summarize the evidence you have gathered to support your claim and explain your reasoning.

Checkpoints

Answer the following questions to check your understanding of the lesson.

Use the photo to answer Question 3.

3. Which of these statements describe what is shown in the photo?

   A. The Southern Hemisphere is in summer and the Northern Hemisphere is in winter.

   B. Both polar regions are experiencing daytime and nighttime hours of relatively equal length.

   C. The Southern Hemisphere is closer to the sun than the Northern Hemisphere.

Use the diagram to answer Questions 4–5.

4. How would the seasons on Uranus compare to the seasons on Earth?

   A. The four seasons on Uranus would be different from Earth's because the tilt of Uranus is different.

   B. Seasons on Uranus would be exactly opposite of seasons on Earth.

   C. Uranus rotates on its side, so Uranus would not experience different seasons.

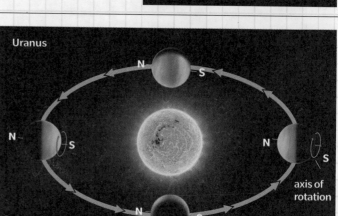

5. Which of these statements describes the seasons on Uranus?

   A. Uranus has two seasons, summer and winter.

   B. Summer and winter each last for about half of Uranus's complete orbit, with very short spring and fall seasons.

   C. When it is summer in the Northern Hemisphere of Uranus, the Southern Hemisphere has no daylight hours.

6. Which of these are affected by Earth's tilt? Select all that apply.

   A. the number of daylight hours in June

   B. changes in yearly temperatures across the seasons

   C. how long each season lasts

7. Electromagnetic waves travel from the sun to Earth through the vacuum of space. Some of the energy from these waves transforms into thermal energy when the waves are absorbed / transmitted / reflected by Earth's atmosphere and surface. The Earth-sun system follows a pattern in which the sun's energy in a particular location on Earth is more intense during the summer / winter.

Interactive Review

Complete this section to review the main concepts of the lesson.

The path of the sun across the sky and energy from the sun can help explain the seasons of the year.

A. How does the path of the sun affect the energy received by Earth at any particular location on Earth?

Earth's tilt and position in its revolution determine the amount of the sun's energy that strikes any particular location on Earth.

B. Explain why Earth's tilt is responsible for the seasons.

Choose one of the activities to explore how this unit connects to other topics.

People in Science

Percy Spencer, Physicist Despite having only an elementary education, Percy Spencer became a productive scientist and inventor. While working at Raytheon during World War II, he helped to develop devices called magnetrons for use in radar equipment. When he and colleagues noticed that the magnetrons quickly heated food, he investigated the phenomenon. This research led to the development of the first commercial microwave oven in 1947.

Research the design of modern microwave ovens. Develop a presentation that explains how the microwave oven can cook food while a user safely stands next to the device.

Music Connection

Sound Waves and Music Music is a mixture of sounds that have different pitches and volumes. Musical instruments are designed to produce a range of sounds. Musicians know how to play instruments to produce the pitch and volume of the sounds they need to make music.

Choose a musical instrument and research how the instrument produces different pitches and volumes. Develop a multimedia presentation to share with the class that explains how the instrument works. Include a simple mathematical model that shows how the properties of the sound waves relate to the pitch and volume.

Social Studies Connection

Mythological Explanations of the Seasons Throughout history, many different cultures have told stories and developed explanations to make sense of the changing of the seasons. The ancient Greeks and Native Americans both used stories, called myths, to explain the changing seasons.

Research one ancient Greek myth and one Native American myth that explain the seasons. Compare and contrast the two myths. Produce a presentation with images showing the similarities and differences between the ways these cultures viewed the changes in seasons.

Name: _____   Date: _____

Complete this review to check your understanding of the unit.

Use the images to answer Questions 1–3.

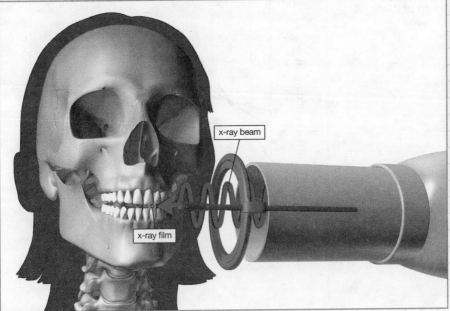

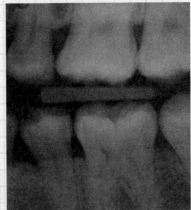

This diagram shows how an x-ray image of teeth is taken at the dentist's office. The lighter areas in the resulting x-ray image of the teeth are like the shadows that you see when you block visible light.

1. Based on the diagram and the x-ray image, what can you conclude about how x-rays interact with your teeth and the tissues in your mouth? Use evidence of the behavior of light waves to support your claim.

2. Recall that ultrasound machines use high-frequency sound waves to form images. How is the process of using ultrasound machines different from the process of taking x-ray images?

3. Ultrasound machines, not x-ray machines, are used to take images of a developing fetus. Sound waves are also used to take images of the sea floor, while x-rays can provide information about the sun and distant bodies in space. How do the properties of sound waves and x-rays affect the ways they are used? Make a claim and use evidence to support it.

Name: _____ **Date:** _____

Use the images to answer Questions 4–7.

4. What relationship can you identify between the latitude of a location and the pattern of daylight hours throughout the year?

5. What can you infer about the difference in seasonal temperature changes in Honolulu, Minneapolis, and Fairbanks? Explain your reasoning.

6. Based on these patterns, what could you infer about the pattern of daylight hours over a year and the seasonal temperature changes for a location on the equator?

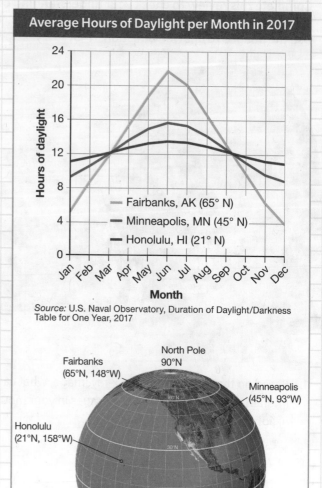

Average Hours of Daylight per Month in 2017

Fairbanks, AK (65° N)
Minneapolis, MN (45° N)
Honolulu, HI (21° N)

Source: U.S. Naval Observatory, Duration of Daylight/Darkness Table for One Year, 2017

North Pole
90°N
Fairbanks
(65°N, 148°W)
Minneapolis
(45°N, 93°W)
Honolulu
(21°N, 158°W)

7. Choose a date and location from the graph. Use the data to explain how energy from the sun relates to the number of daylight hours and expected season in the area.

Name: _____   Date: _____

Will your audience be able to hear you?

Imagine that you are planning to produce a play that is going to be performed outdoors without microphones. There will be 100 tickets for each performance and the audience will sit on the ground or on folding chairs. You need to design the seating area so that everyone in the audience will be able to hear the performers. Develop a proposal for a performance area that will maximize the audience's ability to hear the play.

The steps below will help guide your research and develop your recommendation.

Engineer It

1. **Define the Problem** Write a statement to clearly define the problem you are trying to solve. Identify the criteria and constraints that you need to consider in your design.

Engineer It

2. **Conduct Research** How will distance affect the audience's ability to hear sound? Research theaters without sound systems. How do these theaters use sound wave properties to ensure that all of the actors are heard?

3. **Develop a Model** What types of seating arrangements might work better than others? Apply your research to make a diagram or model of your seating area. Include how you expect the volume to change for audience members.

4. **Optimize a Solution** Compare your solution to the Royal Albert Hall in London, England; the Epidaurus Ancient Theatre in Epidaurus, Greece; or the Vienna Musikverein in Vienna, Austria. How is your theater design different or similar? Based on what you know about sound, how is your solution more or less effective? Is your design the optimal solution? If not, modify your solution.

5. **Communicate** Present your design proposal to the class. Include design specifics, such as seating arrangement and stage location. Explain why your design is the optimal solution. Ensure your presentation includes a thorough explanation of the properties of the sound wave behavior involved.

✓ Self-Check

	I identified the criteria and constraints of the problem.
	I described how sound volume changes with distance.
	I drew a diagram to model the seating arrangement that included how sounds would change.
	I provided a thorough explanation of my design proposal in a class presentation.

Technology and Human Impact on Earth Systems

How do technology and human activity relate to biodiversity?

Ecosystem health and services are related to the biodiversity of the ecosystem.

You Solve It How Can You Compare Digital and Analog Communication Signals?

Compare analog and digital signals by simulating different ways to transmit a photo. Choose the signal type and communication channel, and vary signal and noise levels.

Go online and complete the You Solve It to explore ways to solve a real-world problem.

Monitor Biodiversity

This redwoods forest is high in biodiversity and is a popular tourist destination.

A. Look at the photo. On a separate sheet of paper, write down as many different questions as you can about the photo.

B. **Discuss** With your class or a partner, share your questions. Record any additional questions generated in your discussion. Then choose the most important questions from the list that are related to monitoring biodiversity. Write them below.

C. Choose an ecosystem to research. Here is a list of ecosystems you can consider:

redwood forest   coastal wetlands   grasslands

kelp forest   oak woodland   desert

D. Use the information above, along with your research, to develop a plan for monitoring biodiversity in your chosen ecosystem.

Discuss the next steps for your Unit Project with your teacher and go online to download the Unit Project Worksheet.

Language Development

Use the lessons in this unit to complete the network and expand your understanding of these key concepts.

▨	Similar term
▨	Phrase
▨	Cognate
▨	Example
▨	Definition

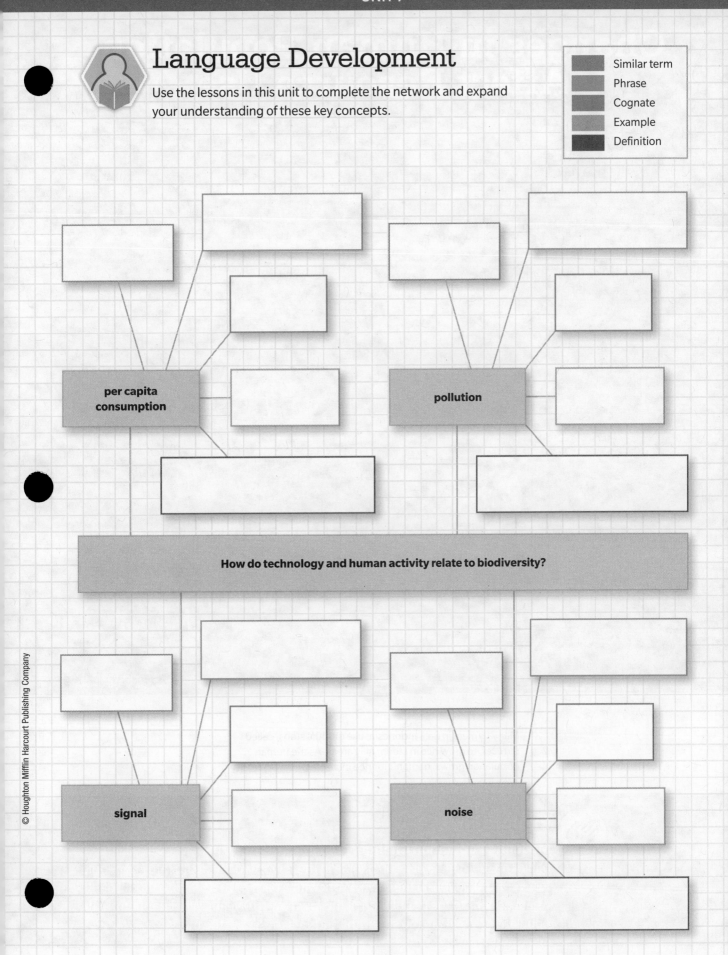

per capita consumption

pollution

How do technology and human activity relate to biodiversity?

signal

noise

Changes in Human Population Affect Resource Use

Many farmers in Bali, Indonesia, use gradual steps, called *terraces*, to grow rice in steep, hilly areas. As the human population grows, demand for rice increases.

Explore First

Modeling Population Change A small town has 100 people. Each year, 10 babies are born for every 100 people in the town, and the death rate is 8 people for every 100 people in the town. Work with a partner to develop a model of what happens to the population of the town over 10 years. What happens to the population? What are the strengths and weaknesses of the model?

CAN YOU EXPLAIN IT?

What might explain the patterns of population density in northern Africa?

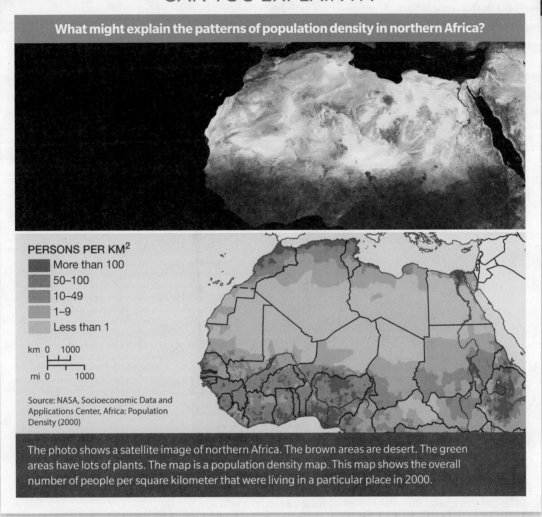

PERSONS PER KM²

More than 100
50–100
10–49
1–9
Less than 1

km 0   1000

mi 0   1000

Source: NASA, Socioeconomic Data and Applications Center, Africa: Population Density (2000)

The photo shows a satellite image of northern Africa. The brown areas are desert. The green areas have lots of plants. The map is a population density map. This map shows the overall number of people per square kilometer that were living in a particular place in 2000.

1. Compare the satellite image with the map. What do you notice on the satellite image about the places in northern Africa with the greatest population density?

 EVIDENCE NOTEBOOK As you explore this lesson, gather evidence to help explain what might determine population density in northern Africa.

Analyzing Human Population Data

How do you think the population of humans on Earth has changed over the past 12,000 years? Think about what factors affect whether a population increases or decreases. Consider how these factors may have changed over the past 12,000 years.

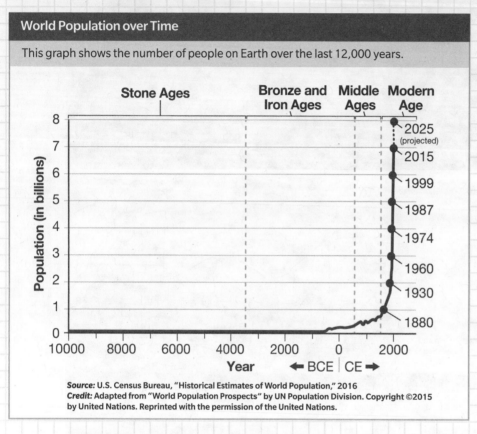

World Population over Time

This graph shows the number of people on Earth over the last 12,000 years.

Source: U.S. Census Bureau, "Historical Estimates of World Population," 2016
Credit: Adapted from "World Population Prospects" by UN Population Division. Copyright ©2015 by United Nations. Reprinted with the permission of the United Nations.

2. Look at the data in the graph. During what time period do you see the largest change in the number of people on Earth? What factors do you think caused this change to happen?

Population

A **population** is a group of individuals of the same species living in the same place at the same time. Every organism on Earth is part of a population. The human population can be analyzed on many different levels. For example, you might think about the population of your school, your state, or the whole Earth.

For most of human history, the human population size was many times smaller than it is today, and it did not change much. However, around 500 BCE the population began to increase. Then, less than 200 years ago, around the beginning of the Modern Age, the human population began to grow rapidly.

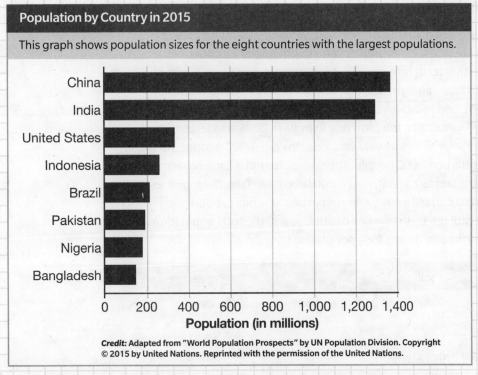

Population by Country in 2015

This graph shows population sizes for the eight countries with the largest populations.

Credit: Adapted from "World Population Prospects" by UN Population Division. Copyright © 2015 by United Nations. Reprinted with the permission of the United Nations.

3. According to the graph, how does the population of China compare to the population of the United States?

Data about Populations

Government agencies measure the populations of different areas, and they measure more than just the total number of people. For example, population data can include the distribution of ages and the ratio of males to females within the population. The data gathered are organized in databases that can be searched and sorted, and the data can be analyzed to make inferences about a population.

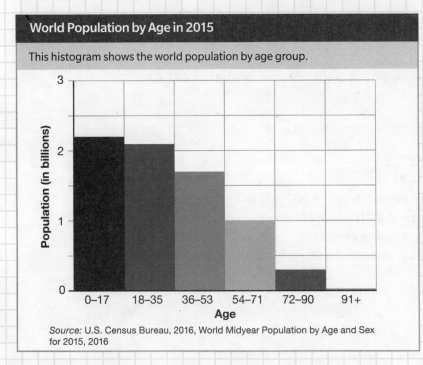

World Population by Age in 2015

This histogram shows the world population by age group.

Source: U.S. Census Bureau, 2016, World Midyear Population by Age and Sex for 2015, 2016

4. What can you conclude from the data shown in the graph?

- **A.** The population is mostly made up of adults over the age of 17.
- **B.** Most of the population that has lived to age 90 will continue to live for many more years.
- **C.** Humans who are ages 54–71 make up about half the population.
- **D.** People are not expected to live much past age 53.

Population Growth Rates

Population data can be used to calculate a growth rate, which indicates whether a population has grown and how fast it has grown. The growth rate of a population depends on the birth rate, the death rate, and the migration of people into or out of a region. Birth rates, death rates, and growth rates are ratios. A ratio compares one amount to another amount, and so a birth rate compares the number of babies born to the total population size. For example, the birth rate in India in 2016 was 19 births per 1,000 people. The death rate for the same year was 7 deaths per 1,000 people. There were more births than deaths per 1,000 people. There was also not a large movement of people out of the country, and as a result, the population grew. Taken all together, the trends in population data can tell a story about a particular region's population. Proportions may be used with the birth rate and death rate and the total population to find the total number of births and deaths for a population.

Birth Rate, Death Rate, and Population Size

Examine this graph to see how birth rate and death rate can affect population size.

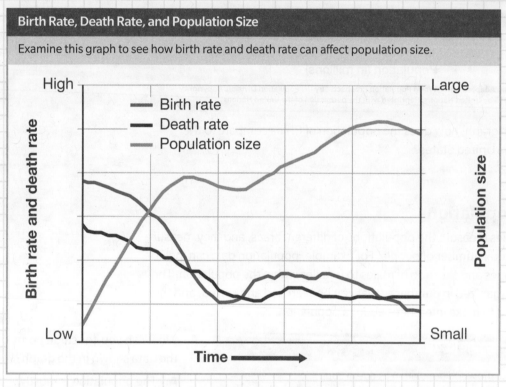

5. Examine the patterns and trends shown in this graph. How are birth rate, death rate, and population size related?

 6. Do the Math A country has a population of 9,507,000. In a given year, the country's birth rate is 11 births per 1,000 people. The country's death rate that year is 13.5 deaths per 1,000 people. Use proportions to calculate the total births and total deaths for the year. Then calculate the change in population.

Factors Affecting Population Growth

Rates of population change can be used to analyze causes of population change and to predict future changes. Significant changes in population are often related to environmental changes in a region or to events in history.

In the data shown earlier, several key factors influenced the huge increase in the world's population over a short period of time. Improvements in agriculture led to larger and more reliable food supplies. Technology and innovations led to increases in planting and harvesting crops. Thus, more food was available than when people relied on hunting and gathering. People invented and improved machines that used fossil fuels, and these industrial developments increased the efficiency of agriculture, industry, and transportation. Improvements in sanitation, diet, and medical care led to population growth by increasing survival rates and the average human lifespan.

Factors That Affect Population Growth

Improvements in transportation and agriculture meant more food could be distributed to more places.

Improvements in sanitation and medicine helped to decrease death rates.

Population by World Region, 1750–2050

Population growth rates differ by region. The last bar shows projected population sizes. These sizes are estimated based on current data.

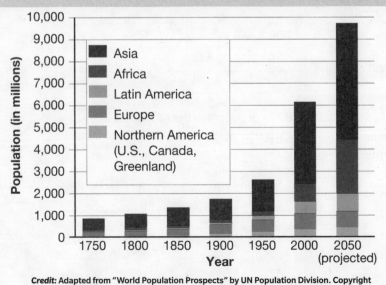

Credit: Adapted from "World Population Prospects" by UN Population Division. Copyright ©2015 by United Nations. Reprinted with the permission of the United Nations. Adapted from "The World at Six Billion" by UN Population Division. Copyright ©1999 by United Nations. Reprinted with the permission of the United Nations.

7. Which of the following likely contributed to increased global population growth between 1950 and 2000? Circle all that apply.

A. increases in birth rates

B. improvements in agriculture

C. increases in death rates in Europe

D. immigration from Latin America to Africa

Project Population Growth

Population data from a span of time can be used to project future population growth. To project population growth means to predict a future change in population based on current data. The table below shows the world's population size from 1900 to 2000.

Population Data						
Year	1900	1920	1940	1960	1980	2000
Population	1.7 billion	1.9 billion	2.3 billion	3 billion	4.4 billion	6 billion

8. Draw In the space provided, graph the data in the table to show global population change from 1900 to 2000. Label the x-axis "Years" and the y-axis "Population."

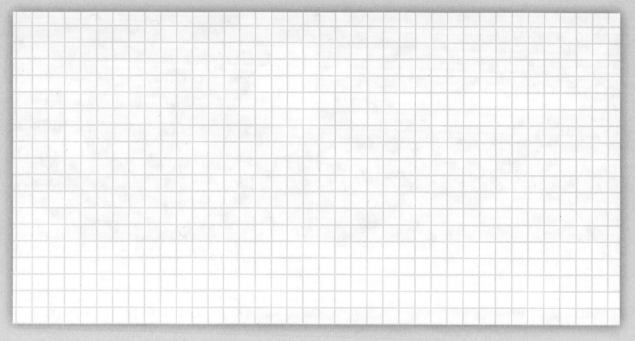

9. Use your graph to predict the world's population in 2040. Include a reason for your prediction.

_____

_____

_____

10. Write Describe an event or scenario that would increase or decrease the projected size of the world's population. Make an argument for why the event would affect the population, and support your argument with evidence.

_____

_____

_____

_____

_____

Investigating Rates of Resource Use

The foods you eat provide your body with energy. Every day, these nutrients fuel your body's processes. All living things need energy, but they obtain energy in different ways. You get energy when your body breaks down the food you eat. Plants use energy from the sun to make their own food, and then they break down this food and use its stored energy. Sunlight is an endless source of energy, but other energy sources can run out.

This oil rig extracts oil from beneath the ocean floor.

11. Identify the natural resources that are shown or represented in the photo.

12. Discuss Together with a partner, discuss whether each resource identified in the photo can run out or whether its supply is unlimited.

Natural Resources

All human activity depends on natural resources. Some natural resources are renewable. They either cannot be used up or can be replaced at about the same rate at which they are used. Sunlight is renewable. Some resources are nonrenewable because they cannot be replaced as quickly as they are used. Coal and petroleum are nonrenewable.

Other resources can be either renewable or nonrenewable, depending on how the resource is used and managed. For example, bamboo and wood can be renewable or nonrenewable, depending on how fast the plants are cut down compared with how fast they are replaced by regrowth. Water is renewable, but pollution or overuse of water can use up clean drinking water faster than it can be replaced.

13. Think about the natural resources you need or use every day. What are some natural resources you need to live? How do you use them in your daily life? Explain your answer.

14. Complete the table to categorize the resources as renewable or nonrenewable.

Resource	Renewable	Nonrenewable
water	✓	
wind		
copper		

Renewable Resources

Renewable resources include plant and animal resources such as cotton and wool. These resources are used to make clothing, insulation, and many other products. Other renewable resources, such as wind, water, and sunlight, are used to generate electrical energy.

Solar panels absorb the energy of sunlight and transform it into electrical energy. The electrical energy then moves through a utility grid to a community. Solar panels can be found on rooftops, in fields, offshore, and even on spacecraft.

The fleece of these alpacas is similar to wool, which is sheep hair. Like wool, alpaca fleece is used to make clothing such as sweaters, hats, and mittens.

Nonrenewable Resources

Fossil fuels—coal, natural gas, and oil—formed from the remains of organisms that lived hundreds of millions of years ago. There were large swampy landscapes and seas at different times in Earth's history. In those conditions, massive amounts of organic material accumulated. Those materials were buried and slowly changed to form fossil fuels. They are nonrenewable, because we use them much faster than they form. Other resources, such as metals and minerals, are also nonrenewable.

Coal is mainly used as a fuel that is burned to generate electrical energy.

How Natural Resources Are Used

The use of technologies and natural resources varies from region to region, and depends on several factors, including resource availability, cultural traditions, and economic conditions. In general, populations of richer, industrialized nations use more natural resources than populations of less industrialized nations do. As societies become more industrialized, they tend to consume more resources. New technologies and more efficient practices can allow consumption to level off or decline.

15. Engineer It A developer is building an office building in a small town near the Mojave desert. The developer is deciding whether to install solar panels to generate electrical energy or to connect the building to the existing utility grid. The grid generates electrical energy from both renewable resources, such as moving water, and nonrenewable resources, such as fossil fuels. If a criterion of the plan is to reduce the use of fossil fuels, which option should the developer choose? State your claim, and support your claim with evidence and reasoning.

EVIDENCE NOTEBOOK

16. What natural resources do you think are available in northern Africa? How are these resources used? Record your evidence.

© Houghton Mifflin Harcourt Publishing Company • Image Credits: (t) ©Thomas Kokta/Radius Images/Getty Images; (b) ©Hans Peter Merten/The Image Bank/Getty Images

Model Resource Use

You will model the relationship between population size and resource use.

MATERIALS
• beans
• cups, small

Procedure

STEP 1 Choose the number of people you want to have in your first model population and set out one cup for each person. Place two beans in each cup to model resource use. Record the population and the total number of beans that were used by this population. Empty the cups.

STEP 2 Increase your population by one or more people (cups). Distribute the resources so that each person is again using two beans. Record the population and the total number of beans that were used by this population.

Analysis

STEP 3 Which of your model populations used more resources?

STEP 4 Use your models to support a general statement about the relationship between population growth and resource use.

STEP 5 Suppose the beans represented a nonrenewable resource. What impact could an increasing population have on a nonrenewable resource? How could you model this using the cups and beans?

Resource Use and Population Growth

Government agencies and other organizations track resource use in populations over time. The data collected can be used to show how rates of resource use change.

Resource Use over Time

Resource use changes over time due to a variety of factors. For example, the use of oil increased as the number of gasoline-powered vehicles increased. To help compare resource use at different times, data can be measured as units used per time period. For example, the use of oil is generally measured in barrels of oil consumed per day or year. The data can be shown using models, such as graphs, which make comparisons easier.

Population Growth and Resource Use over Time

The use of natural resources commonly increases as a population increases because more people are using these resources. However, more efficient use of a resource can also have an effect on overall use of that resource. For example, the graph shows that water use in the United States increased as the population increased for many years. But as time went on, engineering and water use practices improved, and overall water use has decreased since 1980.

The availability of resources also affects where people live. Throughout human history, higher population densities have occurred in areas with resources that humans use, including food, water, and materials used for shelter. Improved transportation and engineering have allowed resources to be available in places where they were not available before. However, human populations still tend to be higher in and near areas that have more resources available for use.

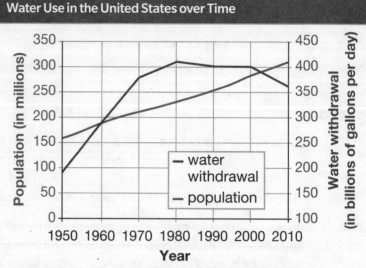

Water Use in the United States over Time

Source: USGS, "Estimated Use of Water in the United States in 2010," 2014;
Credit: Adapted from "World Population Prospects" by UN Population Division. Copyright ©2015 by United Nations. Reprinted with the permission of the United Nations.

Analyze Trends in Lumber Consumption

17. Compare the data in the graph for population and lumber use. What trend or trends do you see in the population size and lumber use in the United States from 2003 to 2010?

_____

_____

_____

_____

_____

_____

18. What might these trends indicate about changes in the use of lumber during this time period?

_____

_____

_____

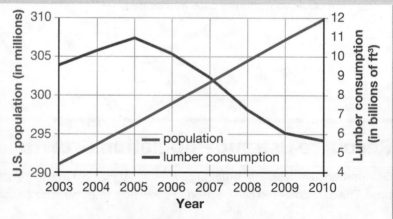

Lumber Use in the United States over Time

Wood that is used for building structures is called *lumber*. This graph shows population size and lumber use over time.

Source: U.S. Census Bureau, Statistical Abstract of the United States: 2012;
Credit: Adapted from "World Population Prospects" by UN Population Division. Copyright ©2015 by United Nations. Reprinted with the permission of the United Nations.

Analyzing Per Capita Consumption

Analyzing how populations use resources can show large-scale changes and overall trends. These overall trends can be used to predict future resource use and can help people predict future needs. Understanding the trends can also help people develop ways to reduce resource use.

Individual resource use is also important. Each individual makes an impact on the availability of natural resources. The use of a resource by individuals, when added together, results in the overall resource use of a population. Consider the group of people eating peaches in the photos. The group will use more peaches if each person eats two peaches than if each person eats only one peach.

Both individual and group uses of resources affect resource availability.

19. **Discuss** How does the way each individual in your class uses resources affect the resource use of your class population?

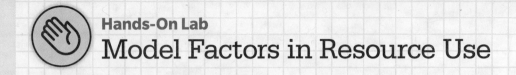

Hands-On Lab
Model Factors in Resource Use

You will model the use of a resource by individuals to determine how changes in individual use can affect the overall use of a resource by a population. The cups represent individuals, and the beans represent the resource. You can decide what resource the beans represent and how much of that resource each bean represents.

MATERIALS
- beans (70)
- cups, small (5)

Procedure

STEP 1 Decide how many beans to use in total. Distribute the beans evenly among the people (cups). Record the results of your model in the table below.

STEP 2 Model two or three different scenarios using different populations or different amounts of the resource. Design your models so that you can draw conclusions about the factors that affect the overall use of a resource.

Model	Total Population	Total beans used	Beans used by each person	Total beans left over
A				
B				
C				
D				

Analysis

STEP 3 How can an increase in the amount of a resource each person uses affect the overall resource use if the population stays the same? What would happen if the population also increased? Use your models to support your answer.

STEP 4 Did one of your models include a scenario in which there were not enough beans to give each person the same amount? If not, model a scenario like that now and record the results. How does this model relate to situations in the real world when there may not be enough of a resource for each person to have the same amount?

Per Capita Consumption

Resource use can be reported as the overall amount of a resource used by a population during a certain period. It may also be reported as the average amount of a resource used by each individual in a population. **Per capita consumption** is the amount of a resource that one person consumes in a given amount of time. Per capita consumption is a ratio that is calculated by dividing the total amount of a resource used in a certain time period by the number of people in the population.

Per Capita Consumption of Cotton

A town of 100 people uses 1,200 kg of cotton each year. The per capita consumption of cotton in this town is 12 kg per person per year.

small town of
100
people

1
person in the town

1,200 kg of cotton each year

12 kg of cotton each year

20. How could you determine the per capita consumption of oranges in your town or city in kg per year?

A. add up the kg of oranges that people in the population use in a year

B. divide the total kg of oranges used in a year by the number of people in the population

C. multiply the kg of oranges that one person uses in a year by the number of people in the population

21. Find the per capita consumption of oranges for each city in the diagram.

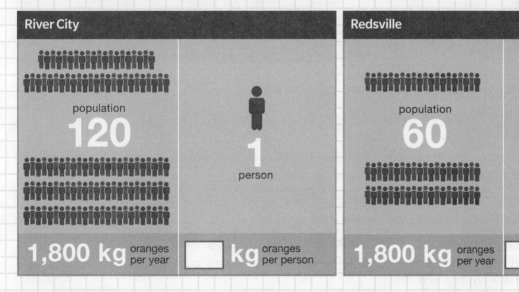

River City

population
120

1
person

1,800 kg oranges per year

☐ **kg** oranges per person

Redsville

population
60

1
person

1,800 kg oranges per year

☐ **kg** oranges per person

22. What factors might account for the different per capita consumptions of each of these two cities?

Trends in Per Capita Consumption

You can track per capita consumption over time by using tables and graphs. Look for trends in the per capita consumption of fish and shellfish in the table and graph.

Per Capita Consumption of Fish and Shellfish in the U.S.									
Year	2006	2007	2008	2009	2010	2011	2012	2013	2014
lbs	16.5	16.3	15.9	15.8	15.8	14.9	14.2	14.3	14.6
kgs	7.48	7.39	7.21	7.17	7.17	6.76	6.44	6.49	6.62

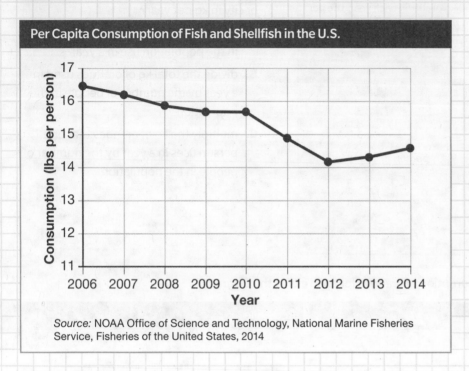

Per Capita Consumption of Fish and Shellfish in the U.S.

Source: NOAA Office of Science and Technology, National Marine Fisheries Service, Fisheries of the United States, 2014

23. Describe the trends you see in per capita consumption of fish and shellfish.

24. If the population stayed the same from 2006 to 2014, what could you conclude about the trend in overall consumption of fish and shellfish?

25. Data show that the population of the U.S. increased from 2006 to 2014. What additional information would you need in order to determine the trend in overall consumption between 2006 and 2014?

EVIDENCE NOTEBOOK

26. How might the availability of a necessary resource in a region affect the number of people who can live in that region? Record your evidence.

Do the Math
Calculate Rate of Consumption

Suppose the population of a community is 10,000 people and the per capita consumption of fish is 6.6 kg per person each year. How much fish would be consumed per year if the population grows by 2,500 people?

Fish is a popular food resource in many communities.

STEP 1 Use proportional reasoning to calculate the total fish consumption for the original population of 10,000.

$$\frac{6.6 \text{ kg}}{1 \text{ person}} \xrightarrow[\times 10,000]{\times 10,000} \boxed{} \frac{\text{kg}}{10,000 \text{ people}}$$

STEP 2 Then use proportional reasoning to calculate the additional amount of fish that would be consumed by the additional 2,500 people.

$$\frac{6.6 \text{ kg}}{1 \text{ person}} \xrightarrow[\times 2,500]{\times 2,500} \boxed{} \frac{\text{kg}}{2,500 \text{ people}}$$

STEP 3 Now add the two amounts together to find the total amount of fish resources expected to be consumed by the larger population. Record your answer in the table.

_____ kg of fish

27. The table below lists resources and their per capita consumption for the same community. How much will the total consumption of each resource be after the additional 2,500 people join the population?

Resource consumed	Per capita consumption	Overall resource consumption (after population increase)
fish and shellfish	6.6 kg/year	_____ kg per year
carrots	5.4 kg/year	
gasoline	1,514 L/year	

Language SmArts

Relate Resource Use to Per Capita Consumption and Population Size

Predictions about how long a nonrenewable resource will last are based on how much of the resource is available and the rate of resource use. These predictions are based on per capita consumption and trends in population growth.

In the questions below, your evidence could be an example that illustrates your claim.

The vegetables shown are renewable resources, but the foil, which is made from aluminum, is a nonrenewable resource.

28. What happens to the rate of resource use when a population stays the same, but per capita consumption increases? Make a claim, and use evidence and reasoning to support your claim.

_____

_____

_____

_____

_____

_____

29. What happens to the rate of resource use when a population stays the same, but per capita consumption decreases? Make a claim, and use evidence and reasoning to support your claim.

_____

_____

_____

_____

_____

30. What happens to the rate of resource use when a population increases, but per capita consumption stays the same? Make a claim, and use evidence and reasoning to support your claim.

_____

_____

_____

_____

_____

_____

Continue Your Exploration

Name: **Date:**

Check out the path below or go online to choose one of the other paths shown.

Careers in Science

- **Find Your Resource Use**
- **Hands-On Labs** ✋
- **Propose Your Own Path**

Go online to choose one of these other paths.

Conservation Scientist

Thousands of scientists work all across the world as conservation scientists. They provide input and expertise on questions about how to manage natural resources. A conservation scientist could work for or with any group or individual who owns or manages land. For example, they might work with a government group, an organization, a business, or a private landowner. These scientists may conduct research about the overall health or condition of an area of land or of a particular resource. They record, report, and interpret the data they gather and often use computer modeling and mapping to make predictions and to identify trends.

Conservation scientists use a variety of equipment to help accurately gather, record, and map information about resources in an area.

© Houghton Mifflin Harcourt Publishing Company • Image Credits: ©Jupiterimages/Getty Images

Continue Your Exploration

The emerald ash borer (EAB) is an insect that can destroy ash trees. It is spreading across much of the United States. Ash trees are an important material resource because they are used for building furniture and other wooden items. Without treatment, ash trees infested with the EAB are expected to die. Treatment is possible but costly. Living, uninfested ash trees may be cut down to help prevent the spread of the EAB.

1. How does EAB affect the availability of resources? If human use remains the same, is ash wood a renewable or nonrenewable resource?

2. In what ways will treatment or removal of ash trees to prevent the spread of EAB affect overall and/or per capita use of ash trees as a resource?

3. How can human actions affect the rate at which infestations of the beetle spread? How would humans affect the rate at which ash resources could be renewed?

4. **Collaborate** The U.S. Forest Service outlined objectives for a nationwide management plan to address EAB threats. These objectives include:
   - prevent the spread of EAB and prepare for EAB infestations
   - detect, monitor, and respond to new EAB infestations
   - manage EAB infestations in forests
   - harvest ash trees—both infested and uninfested—for economic use and to prevent the spread of EAB
   - work to restore forest ecosystems that were affected by EAB

Source: U.S. Forest Service Department of Agriculture

Work with classmates to prioritize these objectives. Discuss which objectives you think are most important and should be given priority. Provide a rationale for all arguments, and order the objectives according to your decisions. Then, compare your prioritized list and the list of another group. Discuss similarities and differences.

Can You Explain It?

Name: _____   **Date:** _____

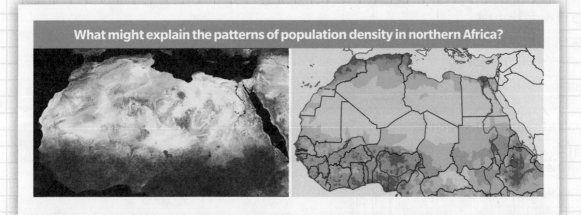

What might explain the patterns of population density in northern Africa?

EVIDENCE NOTEBOOK

Refer to the notes in your Evidence Notebook to help you construct an explanation for what might determine population density in northern Africa.

1. State your claim. Make sure your claim fully explains what might determine population density in northern Africa.

2. Summarize the evidence you have gathered to support your claim and explain your reasoning.

Checkpoints

Answer the following questions to check your understanding of the lesson.

3. Which factors contribute to population growth? Circle all that apply.

   A. increase in birth rate

   B. increase in death rate

   C. new farming technology

   D. improvements in health care

Use the table to answer Question 4.

4. Which statement is supported by the data in the table?

	Population	Consumption of rice (in kg)	Per capita consumption
Middleville	60,000	720,000	12.0 kg
Toptown	40,000	720,000	?

   A. The population of Toptown is increasing.

   B. The per capita consumption of rice is higher in Toptown than in Middleville.

   C. Per capita consumption of rice is decreasing in both Toptown and in Middleville.

   D. Individuals in Middleville and Toptown consume the same amount of rice.

Use the graph to answer Question 5.

5. Which statement about the per capita consumption of yogurt is supported by the data in the graph?

   A. In 2012, each person consumed more than twice the amount of yogurt they consumed in 2010.

   B. More people ate yogurt in 2014 than in 2013.

   C. On average, each person ate about 14.9 pounds of yogurt in 2014.

   D. The people in the United States consumed a total of 14 pounds of yogurt in 2012.

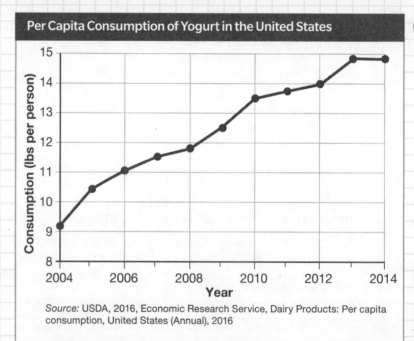

Source: USDA, 2016, Economic Research Service, Dairy Products: Per capita consumption, United States (Annual), 2016

6. In general, how is resource use related to population size?

   A. Resource use is usually not affected by population size.

   B. Resource use usually increases as population increases.

   C. Resource use usually decreases as population stays the same.

   D. Resource use usually increases as population decreases.

Interactive Review

Complete this section to review the main concepts of the lesson.

The rate of human population growth has increased significantly in the recent past.

A. What are some factors that contributed to the dramatic change in the rate of growth of the human population?

People rely on renewable and nonrenewable resources for food, materials, and energy.

B. Summarize how population growth can impact resource use.

Per capita resource use is an average that describes the amount of a resource that one person consumes in a given amount of time.

C. If a population's size does not change, how would a change in per capita consumption affect the overall use of a particular resource?

Human Activities Affect Biodiversity and Ecosystem Services

This coastal community in Seward, Alaska, is home to a port used by cruise ships sailing through Alaska's waterways. This community is located near important natural resources.

Explore First

Modeling Water Filtration Pour muddy water into a paper cup with a small hole in the bottom. Catch what comes out of the cup in a bowl or basin. Then fill the cup partly full of damp sand and pour the muddy water into the cup again. How does the water that comes out of the cup with sand compare to the water that came out of the cup without sand?

Go online to view the digital version of the Hands-On Lab for this lesson and to download additional lab resources.

CAN YOU EXPLAIN IT?

Why does most of the water from the Colorado River no longer reach the ocean?

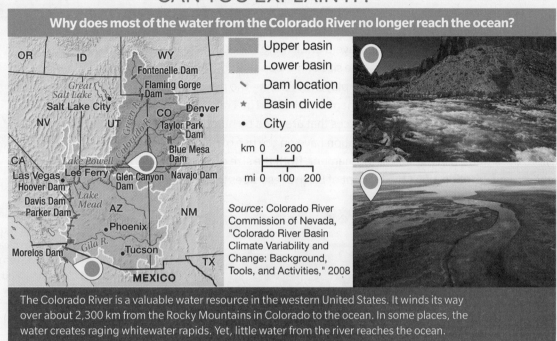

Source: Colorado River Commission of Nevada, "Colorado River Basin Climate Variability and Change: Background, Tools, and Activities," 2008

The Colorado River is a valuable water resource in the western United States. It winds its way over about 2,300 km from the Rocky Mountains in Colorado to the ocean. In some places, the water creates raging whitewater rapids. Yet, little water from the river reaches the ocean.

1. How do people use water resources such as the Colorado River?

2. What are some reasons that a river's water level might decrease?

 EVIDENCE NOTEBOOK As you explore the lesson, gather evidence to help explain why most of the water in the Colorado River does not reach the ocean.

Relating Rates of Resource Use to Impacts on Earth's Systems

Coaches are planning a soccer tournament. They need enough water for all of the players. They will need to supply more water if more teams play. More water will also be needed during hot weather when the players drink more water. The coaches need to consider the total number of players—the size of the population. They also need to think about the average amount of water each player will drink—the per capita consumption.

The water used at a soccer tournament and the land in a rain forest have something in common. They are both natural resources that are used by humans. The impact that total population and per capita consumption have on the use of natural resources is similar to the situation in the soccer tournament. Both the size of the population and the per capita consumption affect the amount of Earth's resources that humans use.

This area of rain forest near Altamira, Brazil, was clear-cut to provide resources, including land on which to grow crops.

3. Which statements are likely reasons that forests in Brazil, like the one shown in the photo, were cut down? Select all that apply.

   A. The local population increased, and more land was needed for farming.

   B. The local population decreased, and less land was needed for farming.

   C. People around the world were using more products from farming.

   D. People around the world were consuming fewer products from farming.

Earth's Systems

The Earth system can be divided into four subsystems—the atmosphere, biosphere, geosphere, and hydrosphere. The atmosphere is the mixture of gases that surrounds the planet. The biosphere is all of the living things on Earth, including humans. The geosphere is the solid part of Earth. The hydrosphere is all of the water on Earth.

Changes in one subsystem may affect the other subsystems. For example, the trees in a forest, which are part of the biosphere, are rooted into soil. The soil is part of the geosphere. The trees are also connected to the hydrosphere and atmosphere, because trees take in water from the ground and carbon dioxide from the air, and they give off water vapor to the atmosphere.

The Rate at Which We Use Resources

You are one of more than 7 billion people in the world using Earth's resources. People and societies use resources to meet their needs and desires. Needs may include food, water, shelter, clothing, and transportation. People in different places around the world may meet these needs in different ways. But, they all use Earth's resources. Everything people use, from computers to table salt, comes from Earth's natural resources.

As the world population grows, more people will use Earth's resources. The consumption of natural resources commonly increases as population increases. Per capita consumption is the average amount a person uses. If it increases, resource use also increases even if the population stays the same. The graphs below show how resource use changes as the population and per capita consumption change.

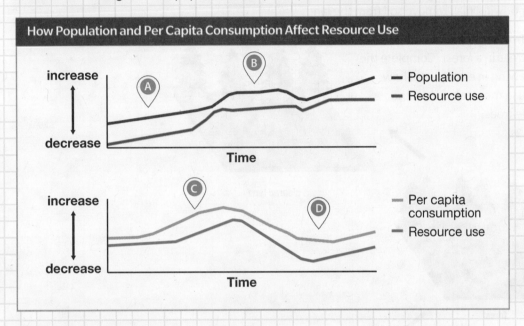

How Population and Per Capita Consumption Affect Resource Use

4. Look at the pointers on the graph. Circle the correct words to complete the statements that go with each pointer to explain why resource use is different at each point.

   Resource use is _greater / less_ at point A than at point B because the population is smaller and _more / fewer_ people are using resources.

   Assuming the total population did not change, resource use is _greater / less_ at point C than at point D because per capita consumption is higher. That is, the same number of people are using _more / fewer_ resources.

5. **Discuss** In a small group, discuss how changes in your class population and per capita consumption affect the use of objects or materials used by the class, such as tablet computers or paper. Discuss how these changes impact the use of Earth's natural resources.

EVIDENCE NOTEBOOK

6. How might the total consumption of water near the Colorado River have been changed by increases in population or changes in per capita consumption? Record your evidence.

© Houghton Mifflin Harcourt Publishing Company

Impacts of Resource Use on Earth's Systems

Clear-cutting is the cutting down and removal of all of the trees in an area. Think about how clear-cutting in the rain forest causes changes to both the biosphere and the geosphere. The trees are cut to obtain timber or to clear land. People may put up buildings on the land. They may also use the land to grow crops or raise animals. At first, only a few trees may be removed, causing only small changes to the environment. Removing some trees can have a positive influence as more sunlight is available to smaller, understory trees and plants. However, more trees could be cut down to provide for an increasing population or for an increasing per capita consumption by a stable population. As more trees are cut, the impact on the environment increases. An immediate effect of clear-cutting is that many living things lose their habitat. Over a longer time, water or wind may remove soil from the land.

7. The diagram shows resources obtained by cutting down trees in a forest. Complete the diagram by drawing in examples of how people might use the cleared land and timber from the trees.

cleared land

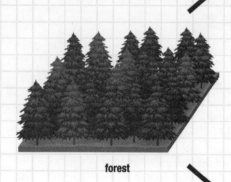

forest

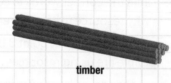

timber

8. Obtaining resources that people use may have

   positive / negative / both positive and negative effects on humans

   and positive / negative / both positive and negative

   effects on the environment. The impacts can be

   short term / long term / both short term and long term.

9. How will the environmental impact of obtaining and using resources change as the population increases and the demand for resources increases? Explain your reasoning.

Biodiversity and Ecosystem Services

Ecosystems can contain a wide variety of plant and animal life. The greater the number of species and the greater the genetic variation within each species, the higher the biodiversity of the ecosystem. An ecosystem with high biodiversity also tends to be a healthy ecosystem. Ecosystems with high biodiversity are often better able to recover from a disturbance than an ecosystem with low biodiversity. If an event affects one species negatively, another species may take over the role of the affected species, which keeps the ecosystem in balance. For example, if pine bark beetles killed many pine trees in a forest, other species of trees in the forest could still provide services. When an area has low biodiversity, there may not be another species to help stabilize the ecosystem.

Humans benefit from the ecosystem services of healthy ecosystems. An ecosystem service is a benefit that humans obtain from an ecosystem. An example of an ecosystem service is trees filtering pollutants out of the air. Plants that grow in wetland areas contribute to soil health. Healthy soils support more life, which in turn contribute to more healthy soils. These soils filter water, which benefits many different organisms that depend on clean water, including humans.

Wetlands are areas that consist of marshes or swamps. The land is saturated with water most or all year. Many wetland areas are lost to human development. This restoration project in the Don Edwards San Francisco Bay National Wildlife refuge is returning abandoned industrial salt ponds to wetlands.

10. Wetlands occur naturally in many coastal areas. These wetlands provide habitats for many species. Wetlands also provide many services, such as filtering water and preventing flooding by slowing storm surges and absorbing heavy rainfall. Humans often develop these coastal areas, by paving over them and constructing buildings.

Paving over a wetland would have a _positive / negative_ effect on the services provided by the wetland. Biodiversity in an urban area is usually _less than / greater than / the same as_ biodiversity in a wetland area.

Resource Use Management

When humans use too much of a resource or use a resource too quickly, Earth's systems are often negatively affected. For example, deforestation leads to habitat loss for many species of animals. Trees cannot grow fast enough to replace the forest and provide new habitat for displaced animals. However, the negative impact can be reduced if resources are managed well. Effective management includes finding ways to reduce the per capita consumption of resources as populations grow. Negative impacts can also be reduced if the activities and technologies involved in obtaining resources are engineered in a way that reduces the environmental impact. Humans can also lessen the effects by finding ways to replenish renewable resources.

11. In order to reduce the negative impact of logging, what could be done to reduce the number of trees that are cut down?

Do the Math

Analyze Impacts to Earth's Systems

The *per capita consumption of land* is the average area of land used by one person. In one town, the per capita consumption of land is 12,000 m². The population is growing. More land is needed to build schools and housing. People in the town must clear land in a nearby forest or reduce per capita consumption of land.

People in the town depend on the resources in the forest to build homes.

12. The town's current population is 4,790 people. The population is expected to increase by 7.0% over the next 5 years. Based on the current per capita consumption, how much land must be cleared to accommodate population growth?

_____

_____

_____

13. Urban planners want to reduce the impact of the town's growth on the environment. They want to reduce per capita land consumption by $\frac{1}{4}$. In this case, how much new land would need to be cleared in order to make space for the growing population? Use variables to write an expression that helps you solve this problem.

_____

_____

_____

_____

Analyzing the Impact of Human Use of Water

When you use water to brush your teeth or to drink, you are using a resource. Think about how much water your family, your community, or your state might use each day. All this human use of water impacts Earth's systems. Sometimes impacts can be immediate, such as those related to draining a wetland. Other times, the impact can take many years to see, such as when lakes slowly dry up. Whether an impact is even noticeable depends on how much water is available, how much is used, and how it is used.

The hydrosphere is connected to the rest of Earth's systems. For example, the water lilies and other living things in and around this lake depend on its water.

14. How is the water in the lake important to the organisms in the photo?

The Impact of Obtaining and Using Resources from the Hydrosphere

Water makes up more than half of each human body. Without water, the processes that take place in your body to keep you alive and healthy cannot take place. People need water to live. So, people need a reliable supply of water. Humans also use water to generate electrical energy, to grow crops, to raise animals, to wash things, to mine and make materials, and to enjoy recreational activities.

About 71% of Earth's surface is water. Only 2.5% of Earth's water is fresh water and it is not always located where people need it. People collect water and direct it to where it is needed. They build dams and make reservoirs to store water. They build canals so that water can flow where it is needed. People also drill wells to obtain water that is stored underground. These activities can affect other parts of Earth's systems and may result in habitat destruction. A *habitat* is the natural environment of an organism. *Habitat destruction* happens when land or water inhabited by an organism is destroyed or changed so much that it is no longer livable for the organism.

As population and per capita consumption rise, demand for resources increases. Negative impacts also increase unless engineering solutions are put into place. For example, habitats in several areas could be destroyed when canals are constructed, unless the canals are designed in a way that preserves as much habitat as possible.

15. What are the possible negative effects of increasing human use of a river's water?

Analyze Your Impact

You will track and analyze your daily use of water. Be sure to include all the different ways you use water.

Procedure

STEP 1 First, research the water flow rates of plumbing fixtures you use, such as sinks, showers, and toilets. On a separate sheet of paper, track and record how many liters of water you use or consume in a day.

STEP 2 Discuss with a partner the sources of the water you used. For example, does your water come from a well or a reservoir? Record your ideas.

Analysis

STEP 3 Discuss of the ways you consume water daily. Record the sources of the water used by all your classmates.

STEP 4 Discuss how water is obtained, used, and what happens after it is used. In the table, record how using water impacts each of Earth's systems.

System	Impact(s)
Geosphere	
Atmosphere	
Hydrosphere	
Biosphere	

STEP 5 How can you change your use of water to reduce your impact?

Case Study: The Elwha River

Humans build structures that control where water goes and how fast it flows. For example, dams are built to serve many purposes. Fresh water from rivers is stored in reservoirs behind dams so that it can be used when needed. Dams also control water flow to prevent flooding. Hydroelectric dams harness the energy of the water to generate electrical energy, which reduces the use of fossil fuels to generate electrical energy. Many dams, including the Hoover Dam, have been built along the Colorado River.

Dams do, however, have some negative effects. The Elwha River in Washington shows several of these effects. Water in the river flowed freely until the early 1900s. Then two dams were built to meet the needs of a growing population. One of the immediate impacts was that the land behind the dams flooded, forming lakes. Other changes to the environment happened over a period of years.

16. Identify whether each effect of building a dam is *positive* or *negative*.

Statement	Positive /Negative
Area upstream of the dam floods and covers trees	
Reduces pollution from fossil fuels used to generate electrical energy	
Sediment stopped by the dam does not flow to the mouth of the river.	

The Impact of the Elwha River Dam

The first Elwha River Dam was finished in 1913 to provide hydroelectric power to paper mills.

The dam kept sediments behind it. This stopped sediments from moving downstream. Sediment is an essential part of the salmon habitat.

The Elwha Dam was not engineered to allow fish to pass through it. So, fish such as salmon were unable to migrate up and down the river.

Water flow below the dam decreased. This resulted in wetlands around the river drying up. A wetland is an important habitat that helps to purify water and control flooding. The slower water flow also caused temperature increases in the water. As a result, oxygen levels in the water decreased.

© Houghton Mifflin Harcourt Publishing Company • Image Credits: ©Elaine Thompson/AP Images

Salmon and Sediment on the Elwha River

Each year, salmon swim up the Elwha River from the ocean to lay eggs. The river's dams reduced salmon habitats by 90%. As a result, salmon populations declined rapidly. Before the dams changed the river, more than 400,000 salmon traveled upstream each year. After the dams were built, only about 3,000 adult salmon returned each year.

Before the dams, sediment was carried to the mouth of the river. There, it expanded the delta and formed large beaches. The dams reduced the flow of river water and sediment downstream. Without the addition of sediment from upriver, the delta of the river lost land mass. This loss of land reduced the habitats for many plants and animals that live in the delta area.

Because of the dams' negative impacts, the dams were removed, starting in 2011. Efforts to restore the river and its habitats continue, and the ecosystem is recovering.

The Impact of Dam Removal on Sediment and Number of Salmon

The graph shows the amount of sediment flowing in the river and the number of salmon before and after dam removal.

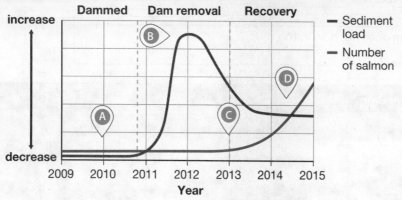

Source: USGS Washington Water Science Center, Elwha River Sediment Monitoring Maps, 2013

Ⓐ The dam blocked most of the sediment from flowing down the river toward the ocean, which limited habitats for salmon to spawn. Few salmon swam upstream in the river.

Ⓑ As the dam was removed, large amounts of sediment (500 mg of sediment per liter of water) flowed downstream.

Ⓒ As habitats were reconnected, the salmon populations began increasing.

Ⓓ In the years after the dam was taken down, the amount of sediment flowing in the river leveled off to 100 mg/L. Salmon populations continue to increase. They are expected to increase at a regular rate over the next 20 to 30 years.

17. Write Use the graph to compare the amount of sediment flowing down the river and the number of salmon when the dam was in place and when it was removed. On a separate sheet of paper, write an argument that includes claims, evidence, and reasoning about how the dam affected the sediment flow, the number of salmon moving through the river, and the number of salmon spawning.

18. How might the impact of the Elwha River dams on the biosphere and geosphere have influenced the decision to remove the dams?

EVIDENCE NOTEBOOK

19. How could the use of dams affect the amount of water in the Colorado River that reaches the ocean? Record your evidence.

Analyze Water Use

20. Which statement about water consumption does the graph support?

A. Water use steadily increased as the population increased from 1990 to 2014.

B. Water use declined as population declined after 2008.

C. Per capita consumption in 2014 was less than it was in 2008.

D. Per capita consumption was the same from 1990 to 2014.

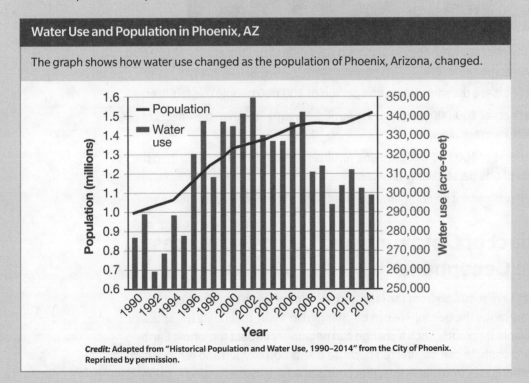

Water Use and Population in Phoenix, AZ

The graph shows how water use changed as the population of Phoenix, Arizona, changed.

Credit: Adapted from "Historical Population and Water Use, 1990–2014" from the City of Phoenix. Reprinted by permission.

21. Phoenix gets most of its water from the Salt, Verde, and Colorado Rivers. How would droughts in the areas of these rivers affect the water supply in Phoenix? Would the water use in Phoenix need to change?

_____

_____

_____

_____

Analyzing the Impact of Human Use of Land Resources

Whether you live in a large city or a small town, you and everyone in your community depends on Earth's systems. Everyone depends on land for food and a place to live. Land is used for gardens and parks. Buildings and roads are built on land. Land also provides natural materials that are used to make products. For example, minerals, including most metals, are mined from the land. Many fuels that are used to produce electrical energy are mined from the land, including coal, petroleum, and natural gas.

Fertilizers contain chemicals that help plants grow. However, these chemicals can be harmful to the environment when they are used in large amounts, especially when they seep into streams and rivers.

22. How do the effects of one person using fertilizer differ from the effects of 100,000 people using the same fertilizer in the same town? Circle all that apply.

A. The effects are the same when one person or 100,000 people use fertilizer.

B. The effects of 100,000 people using fertilizer are greater than the effects of one person using fertilizer.

C. The effects of 100,000 people using fertilizer spread to a larger area than the effects of one person using fertilizer.

D. The effects cannot be compared because different amounts of fertilizer are used.

The Impact of Obtaining and Using Resources from the Geosphere

When resources are removed from the land and used, all of Earth's systems can be affected. For example, the geosphere can be changed in a way that limits the space or nutrients available for plants. Such a change can negatively impact the whole Earth system. The atmosphere can be affected because plants add oxygen and remove carbon dioxide and other gases from air. Plants affect the geosphere by preventing erosion. Plants provide habitats for other organisms in the biosphere. And plants help the hydrosphere by filtering water in places such as marshes.

Many people depend on one kind of fuel resource—fossil fuels. These fuels must be mined from beneath Earth's surface. Many minerals that people use, such as copper and gold, are also mined. Mining causes immediate changes to the geosphere, as tunnels or holes are dug to access the resources. The removal process can add harmful materials to the air, water, and land and can harm living things.

Resource Use during the Industrial Revolution

During the second half of the 1800s, the Industrial Revolution happened in the United States. The population grew rapidly. During this time, technology improved agricultural efficiency. Manufacturing increased and transportation systems expanded. One important invention—the steam engine—helped power the Industrial Revolution. Coal was burned to generate the steam used by the engine. Steam engines were commonly used in trains. Coal was also burned to make steel, which was in great demand for many construction projects.

Most coal is burned to generate energy that is used for making other materials or is converted into electrical energy.

As people began to consume more products and more energy, the per capita consumption of coal increased. Because most coal is mined from underground deposits using large machinery, the increased need for coal had a significant impact on Earth's systems.

23. How do you think the increased use of coal during the Industrial Revolution might have affected Earth's systems?

Resource Use and Pollution

One negative effect of the Industrial Revolution was an increase in pollution. **Pollution** is an undesired change in air, water, or soil that negatively affects the health, survival, or activities of humans or other organisms. For example, burning coal and other fossil fuels causes air pollution because gases and other substances are released into the air. The gases that are given off can cause smog. The gases from burning fossil fuels can also combine with water in the atmosphere to form acids and cause acid rain. Burning fossil fuels also increases greenhouse gases in the atmosphere. Greenhouse gases absorb and reradiate energy in the atmosphere, which raises Earth's average global temperature.

Pollution can lead to other negative impacts on the Earth system because pollution changes the chemical and physical makeup of the atmosphere and hydrosphere. For example, acid rain can result in habitat destruction and the death of organisms. These changes alter the makeup of the biosphere.

Although we know that the technologies required to use material and energy resources often cause pollution, people will not necessarily stop using those technologies and resources. The human use of technologies and resources and the limitations on that use are driven by individual and societal needs, desires, and values. Scientific knowledge can inform people about the effects of human behaviors on Earth's systems. But, this knowledge does not tell people what they should do or how to act. Society must balance needs and desires that require resources with the value of protecting the environment in order to decide how to use technologies and resources.

Case Study: Pollution in the Atmosphere

When fossil fuels are burned, carbon dioxide, a greenhouse gas, is produced. The concentration of carbon dioxide is about the same everywhere in the atmosphere. Humans add more carbon dioxide to the atmosphere than any other greenhouse gas.

Increasing amounts of greenhouse gases warm the atmosphere, leading to changes in Earth's climate. A warmer atmosphere also affects the hydrosphere. For example, the ocean becomes warmer. Increasing amounts of carbon dioxide also change the chemical makeup of the ocean, making it more acidic. These changes can have negative effects on living things.

The concentrations of greenhouse gases in the atmosphere have increased as populations around the world have increased. As populations grow, the demand for electrical energy and consumption of products produced by using fossil fuels has increased.

24. What conclusions can you draw from the data shown in these two graphs? Circle all that apply.

 A. The amount of energy used in the world is increasing as the population increases.

 B. The amount of energy used in the world has leveled off as the population increases.

 C. The amount of carbon dioxide in the atmosphere is increasing as the world energy consumption increases.

 D. The amount of carbon dioxide in the atmosphere has leveled off as the population increases.

The data show that human use of fossil fuels has increased over the past 200 years. It is known that burning fossil fuels contributes carbon dioxide to the atmosphere. However, people can engineer processes, behaviors, or technologies to reduce the use of fossil fuels or to reduce the addition of carbon dioxide to the atmosphere when burning fossil fuels.

World Energy Consumption

Since the Industrial Revolution, the use of energy resources has increased. Most of this energy is generated by burning fossil fuels and biomass, which release carbon dioxide and other greenhouse gases.

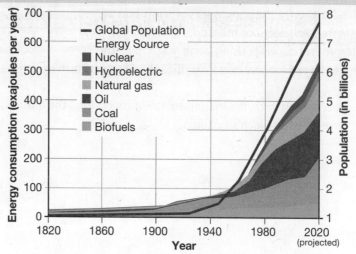

Credit: Adapted from "The World at Six Billion" by UN Population Division. Copyright ©1999 by United Nations. Reprinted with the permission of the United Nations. Adapted from "World Energy Consumption Since 1820" from Our Finite World by Gail Tverberg, March 12, 2012. Reprinted with permission by Gail Tverberg.

Atmospheric Carbon Dioxide at Mauna Loa Observatory

Scientists have taken careful daily measurements of the amount of carbon dioxide in the air.

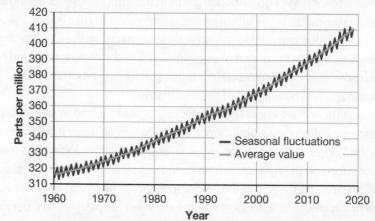

Source: Scripps Institution of Oceanography, NOAA Earth System Research Laboratory

25. Engineer It An individual's use of fossil fuels depends largely on how much electrical energy they use and what the source of that energy is. What solutions could you design to reduce the amount of fossil fuels an individual uses in a 24-hour period? On which solutions are they more likely to act, and why?

Analyze Arable Land Resources

Modern farmers use technologies that were designed to make farming more efficient. Some farmers use plants that have been engineered so that each plant produces more of the parts that humans use.

The graph shows the amount of available arable land and the world population from 1960 to 2020. The number for the 2020 world population is a prediction. Arable land is land that can be used to grow crops.

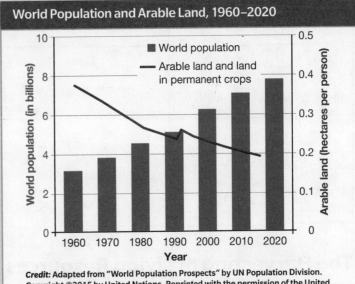

World Population and Arable Land, 1960–2020

Credit: Adapted from "World Population Prospects" by UN Population Division. Copyright ©2015 by United Nations. Reprinted with the permission of the United Nations. Adapted from Land and Irrigation dataset. Copyright ©2014 by Food and Agriculture Organization of the United Nations. Reproduced with permission.

26. Which of Earth's systems are affected by farming? Choose all that apply.

    A. atmosphere

    B. biosphere

    C. geosphere

    D. hydrosphere

27. Describe the relationship shown by the graph.

_____

_____

28. What is a possible explanation for this relationship?

_____

_____

_____

_____

Analyzing the Impact of Human Use of Plants and Animals

Changes humans make to the atmosphere, geosphere, and hydrosphere as they use resources also affect the biosphere. For example, when habitats on land or in water are damaged, many organisms can no longer live there. Pollution in the air and water can also have negative effects on organisms.

Humans also affect the biosphere by harvesting plants and animals as a resource. Harvesting is the gathering of living things for human consumption.

29. What are potential effects of harvesting fish as human population increases and humans eat more fish? Fill in the table below.

A commercial fishing boat brings in a net full of salmon. Some groups of commercial vessels catch tons of fish daily.

Influence on resource use	Number of fish harvested	Impact of change on fish harvest
Human population increases.	increases	Not enough fish left to meet demand
Per capita consumption of fish increases		
Human population and per capita consumption of fish increase		

The Harvesting of Living Resources

Humans harvest plants, animals, and other organisms from the biosphere. Examples of things humans harvest include corn, birds, and mushrooms. When humans harvest living things, the land, water, and air can also be affected.

Overharvesting results when a species is used so much that the population becomes very small. Overharvesting sometimes puts the survival of a species at risk. For example, overfishing is one type of overharvesting. The beluga sturgeon is a type of fish. Its eggs are used as food that many people want. The sturgeon has been overharvested. Now, the species survives mostly because sturgeon are grown in fish hatcheries. When the sturgeon population decreases, many other living things are affected. When the population of a species changes, any Earth system the species interacts with will be affected. Species that were food for the sturgeon or for which the sturgeon was food will be directly affected. These changes may then affect other Earth systems.

Animal Resources

One type of horseshoe crab lays billions of tiny eggs in the Delaware Bay each spring. These eggs are food for many other organisms, including a bird called the red knot. Each spring, red knots migrate to the Delaware Bay just as the horseshoe crabs spawn, and the red knots feed on the crab eggs. However, overfishing of the horseshoe crab for use as bait has caused the horseshoe crab population to decrease. As a result, the red knot population in the Delaware Bay area has also decreased.

Many plants and animals that were once common for people to eat are now endangered or extinct, such as the passenger pigeon.

passenger pigeon

30. Analyze the diagram about passenger pigeons. Why did the passenger pigeon go extinct? What might have been done to prevent its extinction?

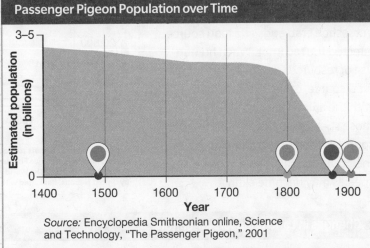

Passenger Pigeon Population over Time

Source: Encyclopedia Smithsonian online, Science and Technology, "The Passenger Pigeon," 2001

There were an estimated 3 to 5 billion passenger pigeons.

Professional hunters began hunting and trapping passenger pigeons. They sold the birds at markets for people to eat.

In 1878, one of the last known large nesting groups of passenger pigeons was hunted in Michigan at a rate of 50,000 birds per day for nearly 5 months.

The last passenger pigeon died. The passenger pigeon was officially declared extinct.

Plant Resources

Trees are plant resources that have many uses. Sometimes, trees are harvested by cutting down or burning large forest areas. These actions destroy forest habitats, and as a result, soil may be eroded, and water in nearby lakes or streams may become polluted. The atmosphere is also affected because trees take in carbon dioxide from the air and give off oxygen.

31. How might an increasing human population cause the changes shown in the satellite images of the rain forest?

1985

2000

The satellite images show changes in a rain forest in Matto Grosso, Brazil, between 1985 and 2000.

Language SmArts
Analyze Extinctions and Land Use

The loss of habitat can have a negative effect on a species. As habitat destruction occurs, there is less space for individuals or populations to occupy. There is also less room for the plants and animals that the species depends on for food.

You learned how the loss of horseshoe crab eggs as a food source affected the red knot. When human use of resources decreases an animal's food source, other species that interact with the animal are also affected. If those species cannot find another source of food or another place to live, their populations will decrease. Some species may become extinct.

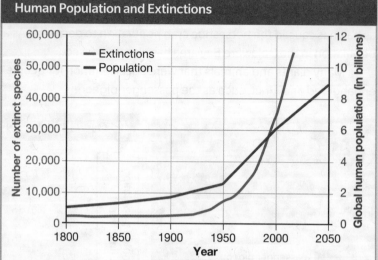

Human Population and Extinctions

Source: Scott, J.M., *Threats to Biological Diversity. Global, Continental, Local*, U.S. Geological Survey, Idaho Cooperative Fish and Wildlife, Research Unit, University of Idaho, 2008; Credit: Adapted from "The World at Six Billion" by UN Population Division. Copyright ©1999 by United Nations. Reprinted with the permission of the United Nations.

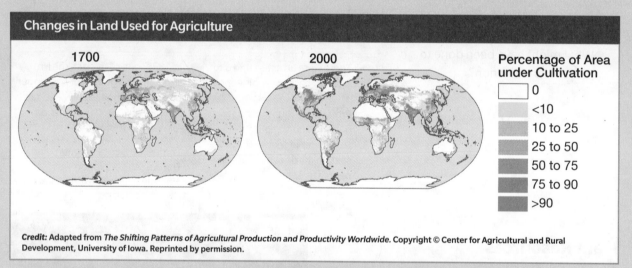

Changes in Land Used for Agriculture

Credit: Adapted from *The Shifting Patterns of Agricultural Production and Productivity Worldwide.* Copyright © Center for Agricultural and Rural Development, University of Iowa. Reprinted by permission.

32. Construct an argument about how changes in global population relate to agricultural land use and species extinctions. Use evidence from the graph, map, and lesson to support your argument.

_____

_____

_____

_____

_____

_____

_____

_____

Continue Your Exploration

Name: _____   Date: _____

Check out the path below or go online to choose one of the other paths shown.

| The Atmosphere as a Resource | • **The Need for More Resources**
 • **Hands-On Labs** ✋
 • **Propose Your Own Path** | *Go online to choose one of these other paths.* |

Suppose someone talks about Earth's energy resources. Which of Earth's systems do you think of? Often, people do not think of the atmosphere as an energy source.

A wind turbine is a device that captures the energy of moving air. Wind turbines use the movement of air to generate electrical energy. The wind's energy is transferred to the turbine when wind turns the turbine's large blades. The blades are connected to a shaft, or long cylinder, which turns when the blades move. The spinning shaft turns a generator that transforms the kinetic energy of the spinning shaft into electrical energy.

Wind turbines are often grouped together in wind farms. These farms can generate a larger amount of electrical energy than a single turbine can. Wind farms generate the most energy in places with windy climates, such as the plains of West Texas or mountain passes in California. So, the location of wind farms is determined in part by the availability of constant or strong winds. Wind energy is a renewable source of energy that is clean. It also uses almost no water. However, wind farms take up space on land.

Wind farms can consist of hundreds of wind turbines. The turbines in these farms are often placed relatively far apart. The land between them is used for other purposes, such as farming.

Continue Your Exploration

1. What are two positive impacts of using wind turbines to generate electrical energy?

2. How might the increasing use of renewable energy technologies, such as wind turbines and solar panels, affect Earth's systems as the world population increases?

3. One of the negative impacts of wind turbines is the noise of the spinning turbine. Near the blades of the turbine, the noise level is similar to that of a lawn mower. Farther away, at around 400 meters from the turbine, the noise level is similar to that of a refrigerator. As a result, wind turbines cannot be put closer than 300 meters to the nearest house in some areas. How does this requirement affect the use of wind farms in areas where people live close together?

4. **Collaborate** Wind turbines and hydroelectric dams use the energy of motion to generate electrical energy. Brainstorm other motions in Earth's systems that could be used to generate electrical energy. Draw a simple model of how electrical energy would be generated by one of these motions.

Can You Explain It?

Name: _____   Date: _____

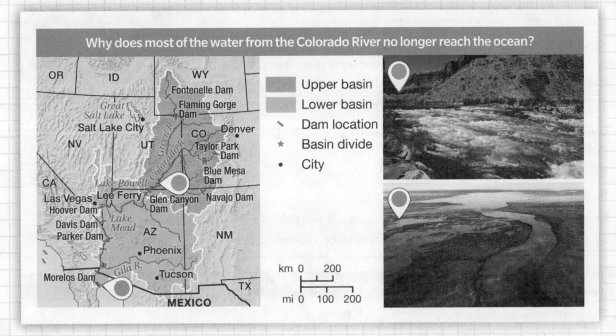

Why does most of the water from the Colorado River no longer reach the ocean?

 EVIDENCE NOTEBOOK

Refer to the notes in your Evidence Notebook to help you construct an explanation for the decreased flow of the Colorado River.

1. State your claim. Make sure your claim fully explains why most of the water in the Colorado River no longer reaches the ocean.

2. Summarize the evidence you have gathered to support your claim and explain your reasoning.

Checkpoints

Answer the following questions to check your understanding of the lesson.

Use the data in the table to answer Questions 3–4.

3. Circle the correct words to complete the sentences.

   The number of cars decreases / increases / changes randomly as the population increases. This change in resource use will likely increase / decrease / not affect the negative impact of obtaining and using resources.

Population Growth and Car Ownership	
City Population	Number of Cars
3,500,000	2,082,500
3,530,000	2,100,350
3,700,000	2,201,500
3,800,000	2,261,000
3,890,000	2,314,550

4. How can the impacts of car use be reduced if the number of cars per person stays the same? Select all that apply.

   A. improving the bus and train system

   B. using carpools

   C. increasing the use of hybrid and electric cars, which produce less carbon dioxide

   D. finding new places to mine for the metals needed to make cars

Use the information in the graph to answer Questions 5–6.

5. The graph shows deforestation decreased / increased as the population decreased / increased. This trend has a positive / a negative / no effect on the geosphere and atmosphere.

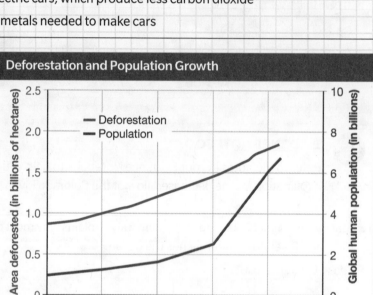

Deforestation and Population Growth

Credit: Adapted from "World Population Prospects" by UN Population Division. Copyright ©2015 by United Nations. Reprinted with the permission of the United Nations. Adapted from "State of the World's Forests". Copyright ©2012 by Food and Agriculture Organization of the United Nations. Reproduced with permission.

6. How does deforestation directly affect the biosphere?

   A. It causes erosion.

   B. It causes poor water quality.

   C. It emits greenhouse gases.

   D. It reduces the population of trees.

7. A town wants to build a dam across a river. Which statements are evidence that the dam would negatively affect the environment? Select all that apply.

   A. It would reduce the flow of sediments.

   B. It would provide more habitat for salmon.

   C. It would decrease the number of wetlands along the river.

   D. It would provide a lake for recreation.

8. An herb that is used as medicine is threatened with extinction. How might human activities be contributing to this threat? Select all that apply.

   A. People have planted it as a crop in places where it is not native.

   B. The herb has become more popular as medicine, leading to overharvesting.

   C. Human population has grown in regions where the herb is a popular medicine.

Interactive Review

Complete this page to review the main concepts of the lesson.

Human use of resources affects Earth systems. The environmental impact increases as resource use and consumption increase.

A. What happens to resource use as a population increases and per capita use does not change?

Human use of water resources impacts Earth systems.

B. Give at least two examples of how human use of water affects Earth systems.

Human use of land for buildings, for agriculture, and for resources such as metals and fossil fuels impacts Earth systems.

C. Give at least two examples of how the human activities of obtaining and using resources from land affect Earth systems.

Human use of plants and animals for food, materials, and fuel impacts Earth's systems.

D. Give at least one example of how overharvesting a resource affects an Earth system.

Humans Use Waves to Collect and Communicate Information

Electromagnetic waves, transmitted between towers such as these, are used to communicate.

Explore First

Using a String Phone Connect two paper cups using a string between three and eight feet long. Pull the string taut and use the phone to communicate a message to a partner. Which waves are involved in this communication method? How do the waves relate to the sound you hear?

Go online to view the digital version of the Hands-On Lab for this lesson and to download additional lab resources.

CAN YOU EXPLAIN IT?

How can a video from the Internet appear the same every time you watch it?

Explore Online

Videos are shared on the Internet constantly. Some videos are watched billions of times on many different devices. Even though a video may have already been watched millions of times and is streaming from a server thousands of miles away, the video will still appear the same every time that you watch it.

1. What are some ways you communicate with friends or family in different cities or towns?

 EVIDENCE NOTEBOOK As you explore the lesson, gather evidence to help explain how an Internet video can appear the same every time you watch it.

Analyzing Waves in Communication

Think of the ways in which you interact with your friends and family every day. When you are together, you might speak, gesture, or use sign language to share ideas and information. These are examples of communication. Communication is the process of sending and receiving information using a signal. A **signal** is anything that can transmit information.

There are many types of communication between humans, including voice, writing and gestures. Communication is only effective when the information being sent can be understood when it is received. When someone is near it is simple to communicate, but how can people communicate over long distances? Throughout history, people have used different methods to communicate over long distances.

2. What do the historical communication technologies in these photos have in common?

Drums have often been used to communicate across long distances. Drums can produce loud sound signals that can be heard from far away.

The light from lamps and lanterns has also been used as a signal. A lantern allows for more control than a signal fire and can be used to send more complex light signals.

Samuel Morse invented an electric telegraph in 1837. The telegraph sent electric signals through a wire. The telegraph could quickly send complex messages over a long distance.

Encode and Decode Information

Communication involves encoding information into a signal. **Encoding** is the process by which information is represented in a signal. The signal is then sent to a receiver, where it is decoded. *Decoding* is the process of getting information out of a signal. To effectively communicate, the sender and receiver must use a set of rules to properly encode and decode the signal. When humans use speech to communicate, the signal is the sound waves that are transmitted. These sound waves are decoded into words that have the same meaning to the receiver as they did to the sender. All forms of communication use encoding and decoding.

Encode a Message

You and a partner will create an encoding system and use it to encode and decode a message.

MATERIALS
- index cards
- pencils

Procedure

STEP 1 Create a visual code that allows you to encode a short message. Write a key on one index card that would allow your partner to decode a message written in your code.

STEP 2 Write a short message using your encoding system on a second index card.

STEP 3 Give both cards to your partner and allow him or her to decode the message.

STEP 4 Trade roles with your partner. Repeat Steps 1–3.

Analysis

STEP 5 **Discuss** With your partner, discuss the following questions: Was it easier to encode a message or decode a message? Did anything about this process surprise you? Record your ideas.

STEP 6 How might you revise your code to make it easier to encode and decode messages?

Morse Code

Morse code was a popular form of code developed by Samuel Morse for communicating using a telegraph. Each letter in the alphabet and the numerals 0–9 were encoded using different combinations of electric pulses. These pulses were transmitted over a wire, where they were received and decoded back into letters and numerals. Telegraph operators needed to be familiar with Morse code in order to encode and decode these messages. The telegraph became less popular when the telephone was introduced. The telephone enabled sound to be transmitted as an electric signal over wires. The receiver then transformed the electric signal back into sound. Unlike the telegraph, the telephone did not require any special training to encode and decode messages.

3. Morse code uses combinations of two pulses of different lengths to represent numbers and letters. A dash (—) is used to represent a long pulse, and a dot (•) is used to represent a short pulse. When messages are sent, the dashes and dots are turned into sounds. Each dash is a long beep and each dot is a short beep. A combination of dashes and dots can be used to represent each letter in the alphabet. Using the International Morse Code key shown, decode this three letter message: •• — •   •• —   — •

A • —	N — •	1 • — — — —
B — • • •	O — — —	2 • • — — —
C — • — •	P • — — •	3 • • • — —
D — • •	Q — — • —	4 • • • • —
E •	R • — •	5 • • • • •
F • • — •	S • • •	6 — • • • •
G — — •	T —	7 — — • • •
H • • • •	U • • —	8 — — — • •
I • •	V • • • —	9 — — — — •
J • — — —	W • — —	0 — — — — —
K — • —	X — • • —	
L • — • •	Y — • — —	
M — —	Z — — • •	

4. Collaborate Send a message to a partner using Morse code. You can hum short and long sounds to represent dots and dashes. For example, to send the letter "C" you would say, "daaah dih daaah dih." Try decoding your partner's message and then switch roles. Record any difficulties that you encountered when sending Morse code messages to one another.

Make Encoding and Decoding Easier

Most modern communication devices, such as computers and cell phones, send information using signals that are not directly understandable by humans. These devices encode and decode information automatically. These devices convert information that can be understood by a user into a signal that can be transmitted, and then convert the transmitted signal back into information that can be understood by a user. So, computers may send and receive electric signals that are converted to sound or images for users.

Waves in Communication

Nearly every form of communication is made possible by waves. *Waves* are disturbances that transfer energy from one place to another. Waves are well suited for sending information because they do not permanently move matter, and they can be varied in many ways to hold information. One common type of wave is sound, which we use to talk to each other. However, sound, like all waves, loses energy as it travels. Different types of waves lose energy at different rates. You might be able to see a light from many miles away at night, but you could not hear your friend singing from the same distance.

Lighthouses indicate the location of land to ships at sea. While other navigation technologies exist, many lighthouses are still in use today.

Explore Online

 5. Language SmArts Choose a long-distance communication method, and explain how it uses waves to send encoded information. Use diagrams to clarify your explanation.

Electromagnetic Waves and Electric Signals

Early communication technologies such as the telegraph and telephone required wires to send electric signals over long distances. It required a lot of time and money to install the wires for worldwide communication. Advances in scientific understanding of waves and electronics technologies have led to the design of communication devices that transmit information wirelessly using electromagnetic waves. Electromagnetic waves can travel long distances through different media and can travel through the vacuum of space. These systems can be expanded more quickly than old systems that required physical wires to connect transmitters and receivers.

Electromagnetic Waves in Communication

Electromagnetic waves, such as light waves and radio waves, have characteristics that make them ideal to use for communication. Images, videos, sounds, and other types of information can be encoded into an electromagnetic wave by varying certain properties of the wave. Electromagnetic waves travel at a speed of about 300,000 km/s. This speed allows for quick communication over long distances. These waves can also travel through a vacuum, making communication through space possible.

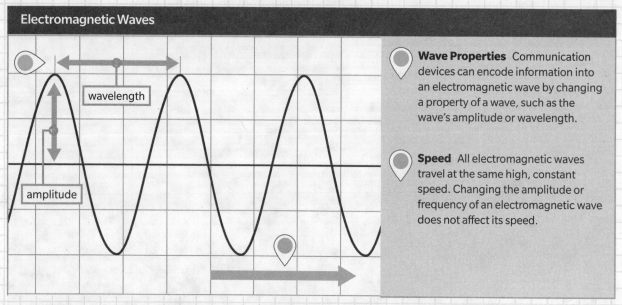

Electromagnetic Waves

wavelength

amplitude

Wave Properties Communication devices can encode information into an electromagnetic wave by changing a property of a wave, such as the wave's amplitude or wavelength.

Speed All electromagnetic waves travel at the same high, constant speed. Changing the amplitude or frequency of an electromagnetic wave does not affect its speed.

6. High-frequency electromagnetic waves usually travel along straight paths. How can these waves be used to communicate from one side of Earth to the other?

Engineer It

Compare Communication Methods

Imagine that you are exploring a forest with some friends. You all realize that you need to be able to signal one another if one of you gets lost. Each person in your group has a phone, a whistle, and a flashlight. Consider the features of each device and how useful the device would be for sending an emergency signal.

7. What are the advantages and disadvantages of each communication device?

_____

_____

_____

_____

_____

_____

_____

Analyzing Analog and Digital Information

Not all information is the same. Some information exists as distinct values, such as the letters in a word. Some information can vary continuously, such as the sounds produced when you say a word out loud.

The thermometer on the left displays a digital signal. The thermometer on the right displays an analog signal.

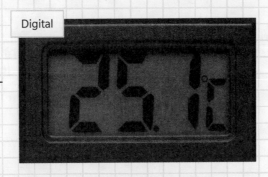

Digital

Analog

8. How many values can the digital thermometer show between 25.0 °C and 25.4 °C? What are those values?

9. How many values can the analog thermometer show between 25.0 °C and 25.4 °C? Explain your answer.

Compare these two thermometers. The digital thermometer shows values to a tenth of a degree. The analog thermometer varies continuously along its scale. It may be hard for someone reading the analog thermometer to know exactly what the temperature is to a tenth of a degree, especially if the value is between two tick marks.

Types of Information

Information can be either analog or digital. Analog information is information that varies continuously. Digital information is information that jumps between values. Sometimes analog information may be represented digitally, as in the case of the digital thermometer shown earlier. The original information, temperature, is actually analog information, but the digital thermometer can only show temperature values to the nearest tenth of a degree. This does not mean that temperature values jump from 25.0 °C to 25.1 °C. In reality, the temperature can be an infinite number of values between 25.0 °C and 25.1 °C.

10. What are some types of analog information?

The mass of water in this glass increases continuously as the glass is filled.

Analog Information

Much of the information we deal with is analog information. For instance, your height is analog information. For convenience, we typically measure ourselves in feet and inches, but your height is not limited to those values. When you grow, you do not suddenly become one inch taller. Instead, you will slowly grow taller over time. If you grow from 5 feet tall to 5 feet and 1 inch tall, you will at some point have been every height in between those two measurements.

11. What are some types of digital information?

The mass of soybeans in this bowl increases in increments equal to the mass of a soybean.

Digital Information

Digital information only exists as discrete values. For instance, if you count the number of desks in your classroom, you would never have half a desk. If you add a desk to your classroom, your classroom would suddenly just have one more desk. The number of desks in your classroom can only be certain numbers. That makes the number of desks a set of digital information.

Graphs of Analog and Digital Signals

Analog information and digital information have to be communicated in different ways. Whether information is communicated using a graph, a wave, or any other type of signal, the two types of information will be encoded differently. A signal containing analog information must be able to show all of the continuous information. A signal containing digital information must be able to clearly show the different distinct values.

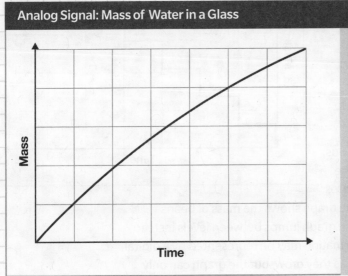

Analog Signal: Mass of Water in a Glass

This graph represents the mass of water in a glass as the water is being poured into the glass.

12. This graph contains analog information. What features of the graph indicate that it contains analog information?

Analog Signals

An **analog signal** is a signal that contains analog information. Analog information is continuous and can be any value. So, any signal that communicates analog information also must be continuous. A graph of analog information will show smooth changes in between values. Imagine zooming into the graph. The values will appear to change smoothly no matter much you zoom in. The graph showing the mass of water in a glass shows how the mass increases smoothly, with no breaks in the graph. Every single part of the line communicates some information. The line does not simply jump between data points. Instead, it moves through a range of values. A light signal, a sound signal, or an electromagnetic wave signal could all be analog signals if analog information were encoded into them.

© Houghton Mifflin Harcourt Publishing Company

13. What do you notice about this graph compared to the graph of analog information?

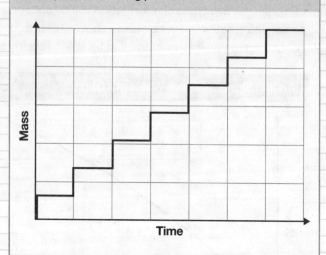

Digital Signal: Mass of Beans in a Bowl

This graph represents the mass of soybeans in a bowl as the soybeans are being poured into the bowl.

Digital Signals

A signal that contains digital information is a **digital signal**. Digital information is not continuous; it jumps between distinct values without being the values in between. So any signal that communicates digital information will also be discontinuous. The graph shows the mass of beans increasing as soon as a single soybean falls in. The graph jumps between levels instead of varying continuously. Sometimes, analog information may be represented by a digital signal. Imagine graphing the height of someone as they grow, but the graph can only show values in 1-inch increments. That graph would be showing a digital signal.

Binary Digital Signals

A computer processor consists of many switches that have two states—on and off. Because each switch can be only on or off, with no value in between, computers use digital signals. Because the signals can only have two values, they are called *binary digital signals*. Binary digital signals are usually written using the numbers 0 and 1, which represent the values "on" and "off." In order to communicate complex information, these 0s and 1s are strung together in a series. Every piece of information that you see on a computer can be represented as a series of 0s and 1s. The code in the table uses a series of 8 bits, binary digits, in the code; this is 8-bit code.

14. Look at the table showing the binary codes for the numbers 0–9. Using this table, sketch a graph that represents the number 5.

Numbers in Binary	
Number	**Binary Code**
0	00000000
1	00000001
2	00000010
3	00000011
4	00000100
5	00000101
6	00000110
7	00000111
8	00001000
9	00001001

15. Do the Math | Number of Levels in a Signal These digital waves use different y-axis values (levels) to encode information. Write the number of different values shown in each graph.

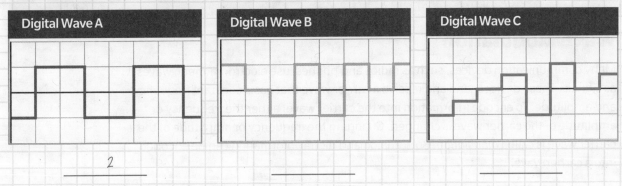

Digital Wave A	Digital Wave B	Digital Wave C

_____2_____   _____   _____

16. Digital signals have a limited number of values. How can a computer, which uses binary digital signals, represent complex information using only two levels?

EVIDENCE NOTEBOOK

17. If you are streaming a video from a website, what type of signal is being sent to your computer from the website? Record your evidence.

Identify Signal Types

18. Think about the different types of signals presented in this lesson. Write at least two examples of analog signals and at least two examples of digital signals that can be used to send information.

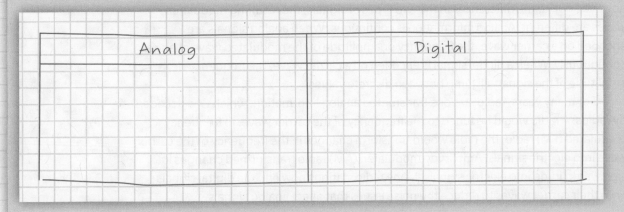

Analog	Digital

© Houghton Mifflin Harcourt Publishing Company

Encoding Information in Waves

Wave Modulation

Many communication devices, such as radios and phones, use electromagnetic waves as signals. These devices send and receive a carrier wave that has a constant frequency and amplitude. To encode information into the carrier wave, either the frequency or amplitude of the carrier wave is changed. Changing the frequency or amplitude of the carrier wave is called *modulation*. Both analog and digital information can be encoded into a carrier wave.

19. How might a modulated wave look different than a carrier wave? How can you determine whether the information contained by a modulated wave is analog or digital information?

Explore Online

A Modulated Wave

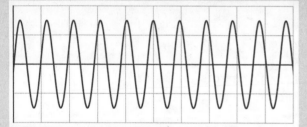

This wave has not been modulated. No information has been encoded into the wave.

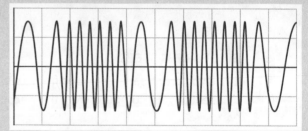

The frequency of this wave has been modulated. Information has been encoded into the wave.

Encoding Signals

The process for encoding analog and digital signals into a carrier wave is similar; however, due to the differences in the two types of signals, the resulting modulated waves are different. Analog information is continuous. When analog signals are encoded on a carrier wave, the frequency or amplitude of the modulated wave changes continuously. When a digital signal is encoded on a carrier wave, the frequency or amplitude of the signal will jump between discrete values.

For many years, radio stations transmitted analog information, which was decoded by radios. A radio would be tuned to the frequency of the carrier wave. In frequency modulated (FM) radio, the radio would transform changes in the frequency of the carrier wave into electric signals. Amplitude modulated (AM) radio transformed changes in signal amplitude into electric signals. Many radio stations now encode digital signals onto their carrier waves to reduce the noise issues that affect analog signals.

Encoding Information

Differences in analog and digital signals produce different modulated waves when they are encoded onto a carrier wave. Look at the diagrams to see how the amplitude of a carrier wave might be modulated with an analog signal and a digital signal.

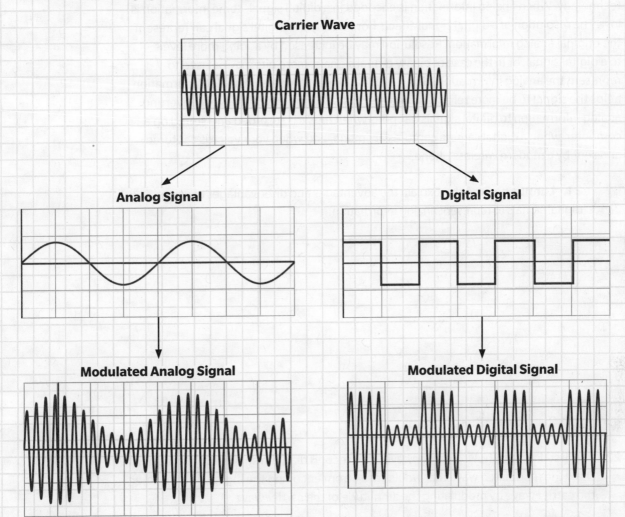

Carrier Wave

Analog Signal

Digital Signal

Modulated Analog Signal

Modulated Digital Signal

20. Compare the modulated analog signal and the modulated digital signal. How are they similar, and how are they different?

Using Digital Signals to Represent Analog Information

Much of the information we collect and communicate is analog. However, we often digitize this information, so that it can be collected, stored, and transmitted using digital technology. When analog information is encoded in a digital signal, some information is lost. The resolution of a digital signal affects how closely the digital signal can represent the original analog information. Resolution may be increased by adding more levels to a digital signal, or in the case of binary digital signals, more bits may be used to represent the analog information. Using a digital signal to represent analog information helps the signal to be more reliably stored and transmitted. This process of converting analog information to digital signals happens when music is recorded and stored on a computer, when a digital camera captures an image, and when your voice is captured and sent by a modern wireless phone.

21. Language SmArts Explain the advantages and disadvantages of using digital signals to represent analog information.

Modulate a Radio Wave

22. The first diagram shows a carrier wave . The second diagram shows a digital signal. Draw the modulated wave that would result from encoding the digital signal into the carrier wave by modulating the amplitude of the carrier wave.

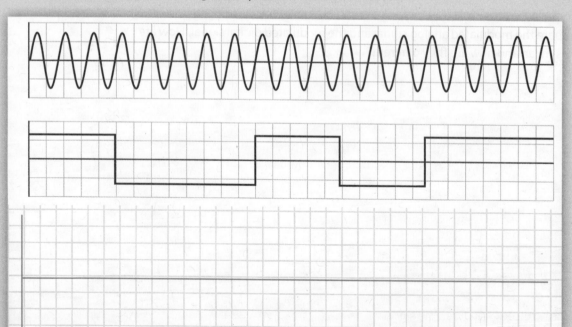

Explaining How Noise Affects Signals

When you talk to friends in a loud, busy room, it can be hard to understand what they are saying. Their voices might get drowned out by other sounds. You might hear someone else say something and think it was one of your friends. Your friends might need to speak loudly for you to understand them. The noise in the room makes it harder for you to understand what your friends are saying, because you are hearing other sounds at the same time.

23. Imagine you are in a room with a lot of noise and you are trying to tell something to a friend. What are some ways that you could improve the communication between you and your friend?

24. Could a similar phenomenon occur when using signals such as signal fires or radio waves to communicate? Explain your answer.

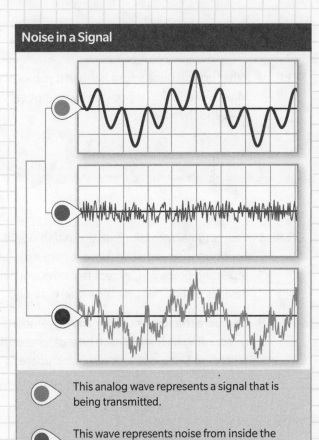

Noise in a Signal

This analog wave represents a signal that is being transmitted.

This wave represents noise from inside the communication equipment or from the environment. The random spikes are formed by the combination of many unwanted waves that form noise.

This wave represents the original signal after noise has affected it. The signal is still similar, but now has random variations in it.

Noise

The concept of noise does not only apply to sound. **Noise** is any unwanted change to a signal. When you hear a lot of other sounds in addition to your friends' talking, the signals reaching you are different from the signals that your friends are sending. Sound from other activities is interfering with the sound of your friends' voices.

Noise can affect all types of signals. Sunlight can make it hard to see a fire. Electronics can interfere with electric signals. Noise can occur any time a signal is transmitted, stored, or recorded. Whenever the signal that reaches the intended receiver is different from the signal that was originally transmitted, noise has affected the signal.

Hands-On Lab
Transmit and Record a Signal

You will be examining the noise that accumulates in analog and digital signals as they are sent and received.

MATERIALS
- two recording devices (cell phones, voice recorders, or computers)

Procedure and Analysis

STEP 1 Record yourself reading a sentence from a book.

STEP 2 Play the message back and record it onto the second recording device. Do not make the recording on the second device by connecting the two devices with a cable. Instead, play the first recording on the first device and make the second recording using the microphone of the second device.

STEP 3 How do your two recordings compare?

STEP 4 What do you think might happen if you kept rerecording each new recording? Make a prediction supported by your observations and information from the text, and then test it.

STEP 5 Your original recording was an analog signal. It was a recording of a continuous sound wave. Now, record a digital signal of your reading by repeating Steps 2–4, except this time, you will use a cable to connect both devices, which transmit the signal digitally.

STEP 6 Compare the results of your analog rerecordings and your digital rerecordings. How did each type of rerecording compare to your initial recording? How did your results compare to your predictions?

Noise in Analog Signals

Because the information in analog signals varies continuously, any noise that changes the wave becomes a part of the signal. Once noise has been added to an analog signal, there is no way to completely remove it. In the final version of the message that you recorded, it is impossible to tell what parts of the signal are noise and what parts are the original signal. When an analog signal is changed due to noise, the information in the signal is also changed.

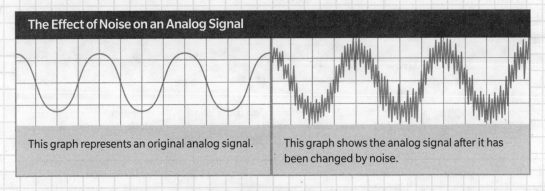

The Effect of Noise on an Analog Signal

This graph represents an original analog signal.

This graph shows the analog signal after it has been changed by noise.

Noise in Digital Signals

The information in digital signals is not continuous. Because the signal has defined levels, noise does not have as large an effect on the decoding of a digital signal as it has on the decoding of an analog signal. For instance, imagine that you recorded a signal that varied between silence and a loud clap. When there is a loud clap, you can still hear it even if there is noise. And noise would not make the silent portions loud enough to be confused with claps. Unless there is so much noise that the different levels of the digital signal cannot be told apart, the information in a digital signal can be decoded more reliably than an analog signal can be.

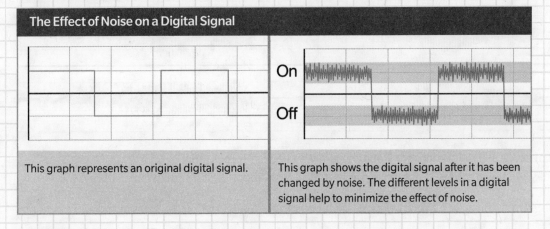

The Effect of Noise on a Digital Signal

This graph represents an original digital signal.

On

Off

This graph shows the digital signal after it has been changed by noise. The different levels in a digital signal help to minimize the effect of noise.

EVIDENCE NOTEBOOK

25. When you are watching a video on the Internet, could there be any sources of noise that would make it hard to recognize the original signal? Record your evidence.

Engineer It
Explain Reliability in Signal Storage

Many methods have been used to store signals. Vinyl records store analog sound signals. A waveform is cut into a spiral groove in a vinyl record. To play the record, a needle is dragged through the groove, causing it to vibrate with the same waveform as was recorded. Digital signals are stored in a variety of ways. Every digital storage method, from CDs to hard drives, uses a series of 0s and 1s.

Analog Storage

These waveforms show two different playbacks of an analog vinyl record.

26. What might cause the slight differences between the two sound waves?

_____

_____

_____

Digital Storage

These waveforms show two playbacks of a digital sound file.

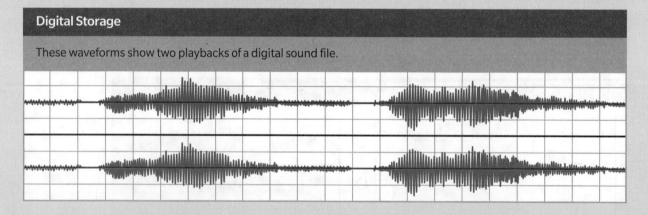

27. Can you observe any differences between the two waveforms? If you noticed differences, what were they? If not, what might that tell you about digital signals?

_____

_____

28. Digital signals have replaced analog signals in many uses. How do you think the differences in analog and digital storage might have driven this change?

_____

_____

_____

Continue Your Exploration

Name: _____ Date: _____

Check out the path below or go online to choose one of the other paths shown.

Careers in Engineering

- Communication Devices
- Hands-On Labs ✋
- Propose Your Own Path

Go online to choose one of these other paths.

Cell Tower Technician

The cell phone, and especially the smartphone, have changed how we communicate. Business, casual conversation, and even scientific study all use cell phones. Cell phones rely on an extensive infrastructure. Landline telephones send information using electric signals that run through wires. The wireless features of cell phones add another step to this process. Cell towers transfer information between individual cell phones and the rest of the phone system. Noise may occur in many different parts of the system, so modern mobile phones are designed to use digital signals. Cell tower technicians help to install, repair, and maintain the infrastructure that allows for cell phones to function. Equipment found on cell towers includes antennae for sending and receiving radio signals, Global Positioning System (GPS) receivers, and computerized switches that protect and monitor the cell tower equipment.

1. Cell towers receive radio wave signals from cell phones and must convert them into electric signals. These electric signals are sent over wires to other cell towers. Cell towers can also send and receive digital data from smartphones. What are some skills that might be useful for a cell tower technician? Choose all that apply.

   A. an understanding of electronics

   B. an understanding of computers

   C. an understanding of chemical engineering

   D. an understanding of how radio waves behave

© Houghton Mifflin Harcourt Publishing Company • Image Credits: ©John Crowe/Alamy

Continue Your Exploration

2. Cell tower technicians often have to install and maintain transmitters and receivers that are attached to tall buildings or cell towers. What might be the advantage of having transmitters and receivers in high places?

3. Cell towers are often placed in busy areas. What might be some considerations when deciding whether an area requires more cell towers? Choose all that apply.

   A. the number of cell phones connecting to each tower

   B. the number of landline telephones in an area

   C. the reception that phones get in an area

4. Cell tower technicians often work on a large number of cell towers. These cell towers form a patchwork to cover a large area. Based on your knowledge of radio signals, why might many cell towers with smaller areas be used instead of a couple towers with much larger areas?

5. **Collaborate** With a partner, make a list of other professions that would require knowledge of communication technology. How would someone working in one of these professions use communication technology?

Can You Explain It?

Name: _____   **Date:** _____

How can a video from the Internet appear the same every time you watch it?

Explore Online

EVIDENCE NOTEBOOK

Refer to the notes in your Evidence Notebook to help you construct an explanation for why a video from the Internet appears the same every time you view it.

1. State your claim. Make sure your claim fully explains why a video from the Internet appears the same every time you view it.

2. Summarize the evidence you have gathered to support your claim and explain your reasoning.

Checkpoints

Answer the following questions to check your understanding of the lesson.

3. A radio tower transmits music to nearby radios. The radio tower uses radio waves, a type of electromagnetic wave, to transmit the music. Which statements accurately describe this situation? Choose all that apply.

   A. The radio tower encodes information into the radio wave signal.

   B. A listener will need a radio to decode the signal and listen to music.

   C. Information is encoded into the radio wave by modulating the radio wave.

4. What does changing the frequency do to the speed of a radio wave?

   A. It increases its speed.

   B. It decreases its speed.

   C. It does not affect the speed.

Use the illustration to answer Questions 5 and 6.

5. The signal represented in the illustration is _an analog / a digital_ signal. The variations that occur within the blue bands _are / are not_ noise because they are random variations in signal strength. In this type of signal, the variations usually _do / do not_ have a large effect on the decoding of the signal.

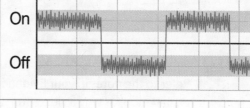

6. This signal is very noisy. Why is the signal still able to encode and transmit information reliably?

   A. Noise cannot change the information in a digital signal.

   B. The noise level is small compared to the change in the digital signal levels.

   C. The noise causes the amplitude to change too frequently to be detected.

In this illustration, the top waveform represents a transmitted signal and the bottom waveform represents the signal that was received. Use the illustration to answer Question 7.

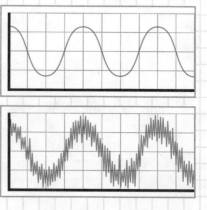

7. Why are these two signals different from one another?

   A. Analog signals are always noisy because they vary continuously.

   B. The process of converting between an analog signal and a digital signal introduced noise.

   C. Noise was introduced by random variations in the signal during the processes of transmitting and receiving the signal.

8. Why are digital signals generally better than analog signals for transmitting data over long distances? Choose all that apply.

   A. Digital signals do not use waves, so they do not pick up any noise.

   B. Noise can usually be removed from a digital signal.

   C. In a digital signal, the level of noise must be high in order for one level to be interpreted as another level.

   D. Digital signals are transmitted faster than analog signals, so there is less chance for noise to be introduced.

Interactive Review

Complete this section to review the main concepts of the lesson.

Electromagnetic waves move quickly and can be encoded with information, making them ideal for encoding signals.

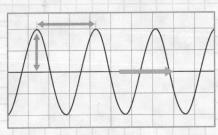

A. What are two methods that you could use to communicate with a friend? Describe two methods that each use a different type of signal.

An analog signal contains continuous information. A digital signal contains information that is represented as a number of specific values.

B. How can you identify whether a set of information is analog or digital information?

Electromagnetic waves are modulated differently depending on whether analog or digital information is being encoded into the wave.

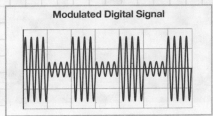

Modulated Digital Signal

C. Compare and contrast a modulated digital wave and a modulated analog wave.

Both analog and digital signals gain noise when they travel from one place to another, but the information in a digital signal is less affected by noise.

D. Explain why noise has less of an effect on the interpretation of digital signals than on the interpretation of analog signals.

Using Digital Technologies to Sustain Biodiversity

A mule deer browses in Yosemite National Park.

Explore First

Surveying Biodiversity Go outside or look at photos of an ecosystem. Write a list of all the types of plants and animals that you observe. Count how many plants and animals you saw, and discuss whether the area has high or low biodiversity. How might your observations of this area change if you viewed the area at night?

CAN YOU EXPLAIN IT?

How can a motion-triggered digital camera contribute to biodiversity monitoring?

This photo of a mountain lion in Griffith Park near Los Angeles was taken by a motion-triggered digital camera. This mountain lion is also being tracked with a radio transmitter collar.

1. What kinds of data could be gathered from photos taken in an ecosystem?

2. What is one advantage and one disadvantage of a motion-triggered camera compared with a camera that is programmed to take an image every few seconds?

 EVIDENCE NOTEBOOK As you explore this lesson, gather evidence to help explain the impact of using motion-triggered digital cameras to collect biodiversity data.

Monitoring Biodiversity

Ecosystems may contain any number of plant and animal species. An ecosystem with many species and large genetic variation within species is an ecosystem with high biodiversity. The biodiversity in an ecosystem can be an indicator of its health. Plants and animals in an ecosystem depend on each other. If a few species disappear, all will be affected. Humans also depend on healthy ecosystems for ecosystem services, such as climate control, disease control, and food production. Collecting data is important to understanding how human activity may be impacting biodiversity. The data can then be used to develop solutions for sustaining or improving biodiversity.

A forest has been cleared to make room for a housing development.

3. **Discuss** The image shows a new housing development being built on land that was previously wooded. How might this affect biodiversity in the area?

Challenges of Monitoring Biodiversity

Collecting and analyzing biodiversity data involves many challenges. For example, animals move and can be unevenly distributed throughout an ecosystem. Animals may also change their behavior around humans. Some plants and animals are difficult to observe from a distance because they are small. Surveys may need to be done over very large areas to accurately measure variations in plant and animal distributions. Often, the engineering design process can be used to find solutions to these monitoring problems.

After collecting the data, scientists analyze it. To get an accurate understanding of biodiversity, large amounts of data must be collected. These data can take a long time to analyze using statistical methods. Computer technology makes it possible for scientists to analyze data and models more quickly now than they could without computers.

EVIDENCE NOTEBOOK

4. What challenges of biodiversity monitoring does a motion-triggered camera address and not address? Record your evidence.

© Houghton Mifflin Harcourt Publishing Company • Image Credits: ©Rob Crandall/Alamy

5. Digital technology and the Internet make it *easier / more difficult* to share data reliably with others. Because large amounts of data must be collected and analyzed to accurately monitor biodiversity, it is helpful to be able to share data with many people to *reduce / increase* the amount of time it takes to analyze the data.

Early Biodiversity Monitoring

Monitoring biodiversity has always had challenges. In the early days of monitoring, data collection was a very manual process that required people to go out into the field to collect data in person. Scientists would collect samples by hand and sometimes tag animals to help track a particular organism.

Scientists often used new technology to improve their data collection techniques. For example, in the late 1800s and early 1900s a photographer named George Shiras III was one of the first to capture nighttime photos of wildlife using automated techniques. One of his techniques was to attach bait to a trip-wire. When an animal tried to take the bait, the trip-wire caused a flash to go off and the camera would take a photo. Scientists sometimes still use bait to attract animals to a location for study. Trip-wires and film cameras have been replaced by digital technology such as motion sensors and digital cameras.

Startled deer in a photo taken by George Shiras III.

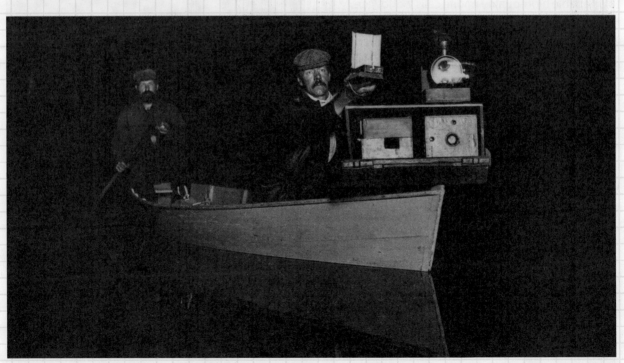
George Shiras III pioneered early wildlife photography in the early 1900s. Here he silently canoes and uses a flash to capture nighttime images of wildlife.

6. Which of the following are limitations of a **single person** collecting biodiversity data manually? Select all that apply.

   A. amount of space covered

   B. quality of data collected

   C. time it takes to collect the data

   D. presence of a human

Modern Biodiversity Monitoring

Advances in technology have improved our ability to monitor biodiversity. Sometimes samples still must be collected in person, and animals still have to be tagged, but technology has improved these techniques. Improved batteries and renewable energy sources enable remote devices to function for longer periods of time. Satellites may collect data, including images, over large areas in relatively short amounts of time. In the past, these data may have been collected by a person on foot or in a plane.

Digital technology has made it easier for scientists across Earth to communicate and work collaboratively. Where data were once only available written in a scientist's notebook, now the data can be digitized and stored on a computer. These data can then be quickly shared worldwide via the Internet. Communication satellites are important in transmitting data for the Internet, but they also enable high-quality phone calls worldwide. Scientists not only collaborate with other scientists, but are now taking advantage of large numbers of non-scientists to collect and analyze data using crowdsourcing. Crowdsourcing is a method where scientists put out a request for data or post data to be analyzed online and anyone can help. This helps scientists collect or analyze large amounts of data more quickly.

Tools can be powered for longer amounts of time in remote areas because of improved batteries.

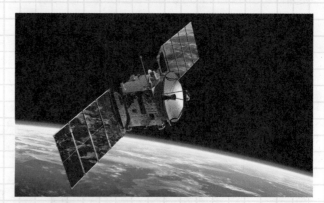
Satellites allow for worldwide communication and can collect and transmit biodiversity data across Earth.

Digital cameras provide instant feedback on photo quality and store data reliably.

Computers and the Internet enable data to be stored and accessed quickly by people all over the world.

7. Match the following digital technologies with an application related to biodiversity monitoring.

digital camera	can collect detailed images of plants and animals
GPS tracker	can collect and transmit data across long distances
satellites	can document where an animal is after it has been tagged

8. Act Write and perform a discussion between a modern day scientist and a scientist from the early 1900s who are studying the same problem of biodiversity. The scientists should discuss the different technologies they use in their studies.

Monitoring to Sustain Biodiversity

Monitoring biodiversity not only gives scientists information about how an ecosystem is doing currently, but also how it can be sustained. Scientists monitor the biodiversity in an ecosystem to see if it is struggling or declining. Both plants and animals should be monitored to better understand the needs of the entire ecosystem. Then, the collected data can be used to help develop a solution to sustain biodiversity if needed.

When monitoring biodiversity, a scientist cannot pay attention to just one organism because everything is connected in some way. And there could be more than one factor causing a change in an ecosystem. Consider a scientist studying a particular species of plant. The number of plants suddenly begins to decrease. To develop a sustaining solution, the scientist must know why the plant population is decreasing. This might involve identifying the introduction of pollutants or other environmental changes or the introduction of a new species in the area. Similarly, if an animal is being monitored, understanding what the animal eats, what eats the animal (if anything), and what is part of the animal's habitat is important. Changes in one or more of these factors may affect the survival of the animal and affect the sustaining solution.

Human activities in an ecosystem may also need to be monitored because human activities may affect the biodiversity of an ecosystem. For example, when previously wild areas are developed for human uses, habitats may be destroyed or fragmented. Humans may hunt species or introduce new species to an area. Humans may harvest plants or plant new species. All of these activities may affect biodiversity in an area.

9. Which of the following should be monitored in an ecosystem in order to sustain biodiversity? Select all that apply.

A. animal populations

B. plant populations and growth

C. ecosystem elevation

D. number of plant and animal species

E. amount of rain

Analyze Technology to Monitor Bird Calls in Nature

Ludwig Koch was an expert at recording animal sounds. As a child in 1889, he made the first known recording of a bird call on a machine called an Edison wax cylinder. This machine recorded sound by carving a groove into a layer of wax and then played back the sound by tracing the wave.

At first, Koch was only able to record birds in captivity. But recording technology advanced throughout Koch's lifetime. By the time Koch made his final bird call recording in 1961, he was able to go out into nature to record the calls of birds in their natural habitat. He used a magnetic tape recorder to accomplish the feat. Magnetic tapes were not as sensitive as wax cylinders to environmental conditions. However, as an analog technology, these tapes were still prone to noise during playback.

Recording technology has continued to advance since Koch's last recording. Scientists are now able to make high-quality, digital recordings in the wild with improved microphones. They are then able to store and analyze the recordings on computers to study and better understand the calls.

10. Technology improvements, including digital / analog signals, have improved scientists' understanding of bird calls because the recordings are longer / more reliable.

11. **Language SmArts** Write an argument that explains how understanding bird calls in nature helps in monitoring and sustaining biodiversity.

_____

_____

_____

_____

_____

_____

_____

_____

_____

_____

An Edison wax cylinder, an early analog device that could record and play back sound.

Koch used a magnetic tape recorder to make his last recordings of wild birds in 1961.

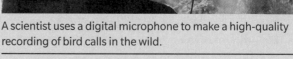

A scientist uses a digital microphone to make a high-quality recording of bird calls in the wild.

© Houghton Mifflin Harcourt Publishing Company • Image Credits: ©SSPL/Getty Images. (c) ©Popperfoto/Getty Images; (b) ©Juniors Bildarchiv GmbH/Alamy

Analyzing Solutions for Monitoring and Sustaining Biodiversity

The Pacific fisher is a member of the weasel family that is in danger of becoming extinct. They live in mature forests in parts of the United States and Canada. They are opportunistic carnivores, which means they will eat a variety of small animals depending on what is available. They are one of the few animals that prey on porcupines. Uncontrolled populations of porcupines may destroy areas of forest by stripping the bark off of trees. In the 1800s, the Pacific fisher was widely hunted for its fur, a practice that is now illegal. More recently, the Pacific fisher's populations have continued to decline as human development and the lumber industry destroy their natural habitats. They are also threatened by predation, disease, being hit by vehicles, and being accidentally poisoned.

The Pacific fisher is about the size of a large house cat and lives in mature forests in North America.

12. What are some of the ways the Pacific fisher population could be monitored?

Range of the Pacific Fisher

This map shows the range of the Pacific fisher around 1800 and today.

PACIFIC OCEAN

km 0   200 400

mi 0   200   400

Historical range of the Pacific Fisher

Current range of the Pacific Fisher

Source: Yreka Fish and Wildlife Office, Local Species Information - Fisher, Geographic Range

13. Why is it concerning that the Pacific fisher is in danger of going extinct? Select all that apply.

A. They live in forests.

B. They help keep a forest healthy.

C. Humans will not be able to use their fur.

D. They help control the porcupine population.

Biodiversity Monitoring Solutions

In Yosemite National Park, the Pacific fisher population is monitored in multiple ways. Some are caught and tagged so that scientists can monitor the fishers using radio telemetry. Radio telemetry uses radio waves to send location data for a tagged animal so that scientists can see where the animal spends its time. Scientists also set up motion-triggered cameras around the park to capture the behavior of the animal. These methods allow scientists to get more detailed information about the location and behavior of the remaining Pacific fishers.

The criteria and constraints for a given biodiversity monitoring solution depend on the situation and the potential impacts on the environment and on the organisms being studied. So, a solution that works for one situation may not work in another situation.

14. The red spots on the map show tracking data for a particular animal. Based on the data, mark three of the boxes to show which three locations would be the best places to put cameras to monitor the animal.

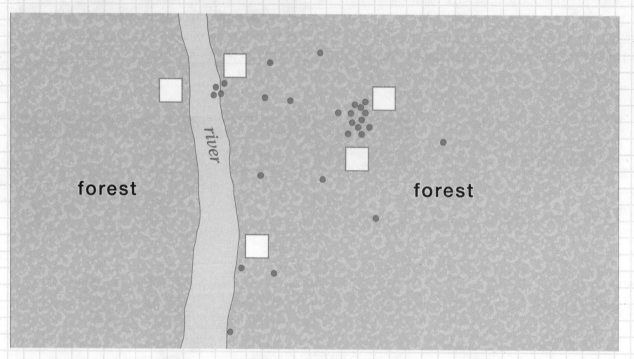

15. Scientists are concerned that a new housing development will affect the biodiversity in a nearby forest. They have decided to conduct a study by monitoring biodiversity before and after the houses are built. What are some possible criteria and constraints for a successful study?

EVIDENCE NOTEBOOK

16. What types of biodiversity data is a motion-triggered camera able to collect? Record your evidence.

Biodiversity Sustaining Solutions

Collecting and analyzing biodiversity data is part of the process of developing solutions for sustaining biodiversity. Park rangers in Yosemite National Park have observed that several of the Pacific fishers in the park have been killed by vehicles while trying to cross the road. Data showed that more of these vehicular deaths happened after heavy rains or during the spring thaw. Park rangers noticed that some of the fishers were using culverts to get to the opposite side of the road. A culvert is a tunnel built underneath a road that allows water to flow from one side to the other. Scientists set up cameras to monitor the culverts to see when the fishers used the culverts. The cameras showed that during dry times Pacific fishers and some other animals used the tunnels to cross the road. During times of high water flow, the culverts could not be used by the animals, which forced them to cross the roads. The Yosemite scientists decided to install more culverts under the roads of the park and put them in dry areas so the Pacific fishers and other animals could cross the road safely year round.

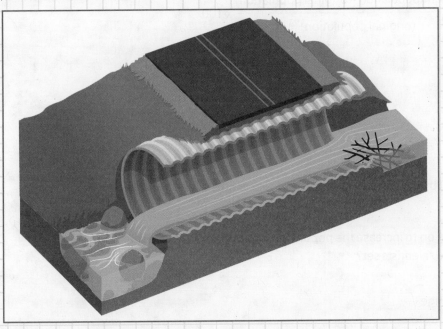

Culverts were originally designed for water to flow under roads, but it may be possible to redesign culverts to also solve biodiversity concerns.

17. How can scientists determine if building safe crossing structures benefits the biodiversity in the area? Select all that apply.

   A. set up cameras to see if animals are using them

   B. compare populations before and after

   C. use structures that are successful elsewhere

   D. measure to see if they are big enough for animals

18. Explain why you chose your answers.

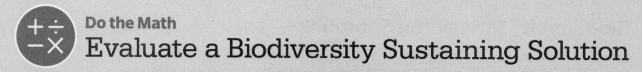

Do the Math

Evaluate a Biodiversity Sustaining Solution

Suppose that scientists have been monitoring the biodiversity of a desert ecosystem. They noticed that the population of prickly pear cactus is much lower now than it was 20 years ago. Scientists determined that an acceptable sustaining solution would increase the population of prickly pear cactus by 5–10% in the next year. When the study began, the population of prickly pear cactus in an area was 100. After a year of implementing the solution and monitoring the population of prickly pear cacti, the population increased to 120.

19. Calculate the percent growth of the prickly pear cactus population and determine if it falls within the acceptable increase the scientists set.

$$\text{percent change} = \frac{(\text{current population} - \text{original population})}{(\text{original population})} \times 100$$

The percent change of the population of the prickly pear cactus was _____.

20. Did the sustaining solution to increase the population of prickly pear cactus satisfy the growth criterion the scientists set?

A. No, it was too low.

B. Yes, it fell in their range.

C. No, it was too high.

D. Yes, it was higher, but that is ok.

21. Increasing the population of an organism can be positive for the biodiversity of an ecosystem. Can too much growth in a population be bad for the biodiversity in an area? Explain.

© Houghton Mifflin Harcourt Publishing Company

Developing Solutions for Monitoring Biodiversity

The Engineering Design Process

The engineering design process (EDP) may be used to find solutions to a wide variety of problems. Problems may be as simple as keeping a glass of water cold or as complex as monitoring the biodiversity in an area. The EDP has many steps, and the steps may be repeated or revisited as you work toward finding a solution for the problem. And while the process follows the same steps regardless of the problem, the results of the steps depend on the particular problem you are trying to solve.

A scientist collects water quality data using digital technology.

One important aspect of developing solutions for almost any problem is collecting reliable data. Digital technology has improved scientists' ability to collect, store, and analyze data reliably.

22. Why are reliable data important for the EDP to be successful?

Identify the Problem

When it comes to biodiversity, the first problem that must be solved is how to monitor biodiversity in a particular area. After a solution for monitoring biodiversity is developed and implemented, the collected data can be used to determine if biodiversity is threatened. If it is, the problem shifts from monitoring to sustaining biodiversity, with different criteria and constraints. The declining fisher populations, described previously, are an example of a problem shifting from monitoring biodiversity to sustaining biodiversity. After a solution is implemented, the problem shifts back to monitoring to see if the solution has worked.

Monitoring biodiversity is a complex issue, so a monitoring solution may only monitor a small part of an ecosystem. When identifying a problem, the problem statement should be as specific as possible. Writing a problem like "I want to monitor seals," is not helpful for designing a solution. What about the seals needs to be monitored? Do you want to monitor their health, their movement, or their breeding habits? A better, more specific problem could be written as, "I want to measure the population of harbor seals within 25 kilometers of the California Channel Islands."

After the problem is identified, research should be done to see how similar problems have been solved in the past. Research also involves gathering existing data about the problem. This research can then be used to refine the problem statement before further defining the problem by identifying criteria and constraints.

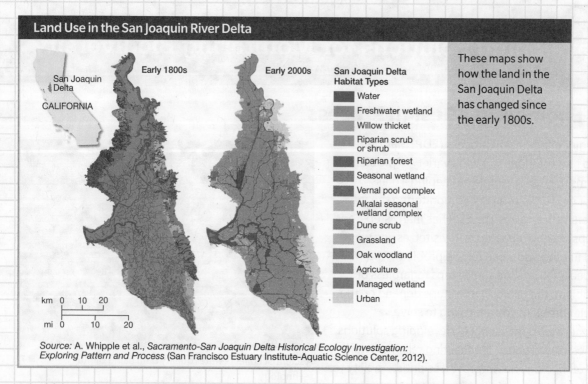

Land Use in the San Joaquin River Delta

CALIFORNIA
San Joaquin Delta

Early 1800s

Early 2000s

San Joaquin Delta Habitat Types
- Water
- Freshwater wetland
- Willow thicket
- Riparian scrub or shrub
- Riparian forest
- Seasonal wetland
- Vernal pool complex
- Alkalai seasonal wetland complex
- Dune scrub
- Grassland
- Oak woodland
- Agriculture
- Managed wetland
- Urban

These maps show how the land in the San Joaquin Delta has changed since the early 1800s.

km 0 10 20
mi 0 10 20

Source: A. Whipple et al., *Sacramento-San Joaquin Delta Historical Ecology Investigation: Exploring Pattern and Process* (San Francisco Estuary Institute-Aquatic Science Center, 2012).

23. **Discuss** Look at the maps and discuss how the changing land use might affect biodiversity in the deltas. With a group, generate as many questions as possible related to the problem of monitoring biodiversity in the deltas. Then, select the question you think best identifies the problem you would investigate.

Define the Problem

Defining a problem involves identifying the criteria and constraints specific to the problem. Remember, criteria are the desired features of the solution. Criteria might include the type of data needed. Constraints are limitations or obstacles that must be overcome to develop an acceptable solution. Constraints may involve time limits, budget concerns, and the laws of physics. The criteria and constraints should be specific. When solutions are brainstormed and tested, they are judged against the criteria and constraints of the problem.

A constraint for a study monitoring the biodiversity of this area might be that the interactions of the sea lions and the cormorants should not be affected by the study.

Identify Criteria and Constraints

Problems may have any number of criteria and constraints. Consider the problem of monitoring seals. Seals spend much of their life underwater in the ocean, but sometimes sun themselves on rocks or shorelines. The criteria for this monitoring problem should specify if the monitoring will include both underwater and above water monitoring and what other types of data the solution should provide. Constraints include making sure the chosen technology can be used in saltwater if underwater measurements are desired.

24. Which of the following constraints apply to the problem of monitoring seals? Select all that apply.
    A. transmit in saltwater
    B. waterproof
    C. withstand high pressure
    D. work at high altitudes
    E. withstand dry climate
    F. work in low amounts of light

Rank Criteria

When it is not possible to find a solution that satisfies all of a problem's criteria within the constraints, tradeoffs must be made. Sometimes multiple solutions may satisfy all of the criteria. To help choose the best design, engineers must decide the importance of each criterion relative to the other criteria. The design that better satisfies the more important criteria is the more desirable solution.

25. Which of the following two criteria related to monitoring seals is more important? Explain your reasoning. Solution A collects data about seal behavior 24 hours a day. Solution B collects data for at least three months.

Case Study: Monitor a Kelp Forest

Sea kelp forests off the coast of California provide food and shelter to many marine organisms. If scientists were to monitor the health of the sea kelp forests, what criteria would need to be met, and what constraints would they have? Some criteria might be that the solution measures the average length of a strand of kelp, the amount of pollution in the area, and the number of other plants growing in the area. Constraints for this problem could include that the technology used must work in saltwater and the amount of time and people it will take to measure the kelp along the many miles of California coastline.

Long strands of kelp form an underwater forest. Many animals rely on kelp forests for protection and food.

Hands-On Lab
Brainstorm and Evaluate Solutions for Monitoring Biodiversity

You will develop criteria and constraints and then brainstorm and evaluate possible solutions for monitoring marine biodiversity in a coastal area.

A city is concerned about the marine biodiversity in a nearby coastal area. Your job is to present a possible solution to the city for monitoring biodiversity.

MATERIALS
- computer for research
- paper
- pencil

Criteria	Constraints
• provides data about the types and numbers of plant life	• solution works in an ocean environment
• provides data about the types and numbers of animal life	• solution requires no more than two scientists for data collection
• data can be stored on a computer for analysis	
• collects data over a six-month time period	

Procedure and Analysis

STEP 1 Research current and past methods for monitoring biodiversity.

STEP 2 With a partner, study the criteria and constraints listed. Decide whether to add to them or change them before continuing. Consider scientific principles and impacts on the environment that might limit possible solutions.

STEP 3 Brainstorm possible solutions for monitoring biodiversity in a coastal area. Record these on a separate piece of paper.

STEP 4 Choose the three most promising solutions, based on your knowledge, to analyze in more detail. Write a short description of the three solutions.

STEP 5 Complete a decision matrix to compare your three most promising solutions from Step 4. Give each criterion a rating from 1-5, with 5 being the most important. Multiple criteria may have the same rating. Then give each design a score between 1 and the maximum value for each criterion. In other words, the maximum value that can be used for each score is equal to the criterion rating. Sum the scores for each design. The design with the highest total score is likely to be the most promising. If you made changes to the criteria in Step 2, make your decision matrix on a separate piece of paper.

Criterion	Criterion rating (1-5)	Design 1 score	Design 2 score	Design 3 score
Provides data about the types and numbers of plant life				
Provides data about the types and numbers of animal life				
Data can be stored on a computer for analysis				
Collects data over a six-month time period				
Total score				

STEP 6 Evaluate and choose a solution. You may choose to combine two or more solutions to create a better solution. Describe your chosen solution.

STEP 7 Present your solution for monitoring biodiversity in a coastal area to your class. Include a visual display in your presentation.

Compare Animal Tracking Requirements

Tracking devices are invaluable for biodiversity monitoring. Motion triggered cameras only capture a moment in time while GPS trackers can capture information for many days about an animal. When tagging an animal, the device should not interfere with the animal's daily life. For this reason, tracking devices are more commonly used with large animals, because larger animals can carry more weight without it affecting their daily life. Consider how the tracker used on a grizzly bear needs to be different from one used on a tiger shark.

The GPS trackers on a shark attaches to its dorsal fin.

Bears may wear GPS trackers on collars around their necks.

26. Which of the criteria and constraints apply to tracking devices designed for tracking a shark, bear, or both?

    A. can transmit through salt water _____

    B. can transmit over long distances _____

    C. is resistant to ultraviolet light from sunlight _____

    D. will not fall off during expected activities _____

    E. is not corroded by salt water _____

27. **Language SmArts** Tracking devices can collect not only the location, but also other data, such as temperature or pressure, from the environment around the tagged animal. Devices may transmit these data along with the tracking information, or the data may be stored locally on the device to be collected later. Storing the data locally extends the battery life, but the data must be manually retrieved later. Make an argument for which option you would choose.

_____

_____

_____

_____

_____

_____

Continue Your Exploration

Name: _____ **Date:** _____

Check out the path below or go online to choose one of the other paths shown.

People in Science

- **Motion Sensors**
- **Hands-On Labs** 🖐
- **Propose Your Own Path**

Go online to choose one of these other paths

Kathryn Purcell, Biologist

Dr. Kathryn Purcell is a research wildlife biologist who focuses on how to maintain animal populations. She has always had an interest in biology and has a Ph.D. in Ecology, Evolution, and Conservation Biology from the University of Nevada, Reno.

The western pond turtle is a reptile that spends much of its life in water. From 2009 to 2015, Purcell and her team studied a small population of western pond turtles near a stock pond in the San Joaquin Experimental Range in Madera County, CA. The stock pond in the area is not fed by a stream or creek. During years with normal precipitation, the pond fills with enough rainfall runoff during the wet winter months to last year-round, despite losing water to evaporation during the hot, dry summers. During the years of the study, the region was hit by a long and sustained drought. The pond dried up completely early in the summer or toward the end of summer, depending on the amount of winter precipitation.

Purcell and her team tracked the turtles' locations and then gathered additional data about the turtles' behavior. All of the tagged turtles survived during years of normal precipitation. During drought years when there was very little precipitation, many of the turtles died, and those that did survive showed unusual behaviors. Some turtles traveled long distances to find new sources of water. Another turtle ended up living completely on land for almost two years, which had never been observed before for this species of turtle. This turtle ended up in a water trough for livestock.

Kathryn Purcell shows a western pond turtle tagged with a radio transmitter.

A western pond turtle suns itself near the edge of a pond.

Continue Your Exploration

1. What effects did the drought have on the western pond turtle population?

   A. the population decreased

   B. the population increased

   C. the population did not change

Dr. Purcell and her team attached radio transmitters to the turtles, and then they used hand-held receivers to track the locations of the tagged turtles. To tag the turtles, each turtle needed to be trapped first. Each transmitter had a life span of up to two years. Sometimes the transmitters fell off or stopped working, and then the data from those transmitters could not be included in the study.

2. Compare this method of monitoring the turtles to other possible methods. What are the benefits and drawbacks of this method compared to other methods?

3. The tracking data are only part of the monitoring story. What other data are needed to know how drought affects the western pond turtle?

4. How can the turtle tracking data be used to develop a solution to help sustain similar species in future droughts?

5. **Collaborate** With a partner, discuss what solutions could be implemented to help with the populations of western pond turtles during times of drought.

Can You Explain It?

Name: _____   Date: _____

How can a motion-triggered digital camera contribute to biodiversity monitoring?

 EVIDENCE NOTEBOOK

Refer to the notes in your Evidence Notebook to help you construct an explanation of how motion-triggered digital cameras contribute to biodiversity monitoring.

1. State your claim. Make sure your claim fully explains how motion-triggered digital cameras contribute to biodiversity monitoring.

2. Summarize the evidence you have gathered to support your claim and explain your reasoning.

Checkpoints

Answer the following questions to check your understanding of the lesson.

Use the photo to answer Question 3.

3. Which of the following would minimize the impact of the road on biodiversity in the area shown in the photo? Select all that apply.

   A. Add bridges or tunnels to help animals safely cross the road.

   B. Paint the road green so it blends in with the surroundings.

   C. Set a low speed limit and add speed bumps to slow traffic.

   D. Increase the road size by adding lanes.

Use the graph to answer Questions 4 and 5

4. When the population of species 1 increases, species 3 increases / decreases / does not change.

5. Which of the statements are true, based on the graph?

   A. Biodiversity in the area is increasing.

   B. Biodiversity in the area is decreasing.

   C. More data are needed to describe the biodiversity in the area.

   D. An increase in species 1 is causing species 2 and species 3 to decrease.

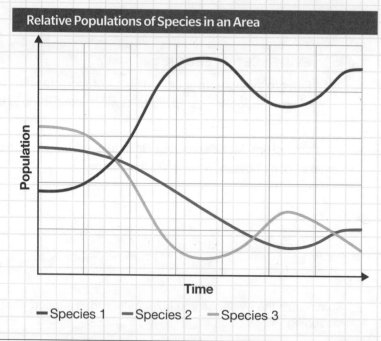

Relative Populations of Species in an Area

Population

Time

▬Species 1 ▬Species 2 ▬Species 3

6. Digital technology has improved / not changed scientists' ability to monitor biodiversity. Compared to analog data, digital data are more / less reliable because they are more / less sensitive to noise when stored, transmitted, or accessed. Biodiversity data must be collected in nature where noise is / is not expected.

7. Engineers and scientists choose solutions for biodiversity problems based on their opinion / criteria and constraints. A solution is / is not influenced by society.

Interactive Review

Complete this section to review the main concepts of the lesson.

Advances in technology have helped scientists collect and analyze biodiversity data to develop solutions to sustain biodiversity.

A. Explain how digital technologies have impacted the ways that scientists collect and analyze biodiversity data.

Solutions for monitoring and sustaining biodiversity vary and must be evaluated against their own unique requirements.

B. Scientists are concerned about the biodiversity in a forested area. Can the same technologies and methods be used to monitor both plant and animal life? Explain why or why not.

The engineering design process is helpful for developing solutions to monitor and/or sustain biodiversity.

C. Scientists want to track a deer and a squirrel using a GPS tracker. How are the constraints for these monitoring problems different?

Choose one of the activities to explore how this unit connects to other topics.

☐ People in Science

Dr. Dolly Garza, Marine Advisory Agent
Traditional knowledge of ecology from her Native Alaskan community and studies of fisheries and marine resources both inform Dr. Garza's work as a Marine Advisory Agent. She uses her knowledge of sustainable practices in her work as a community educator, a policy advisor, and a spokesperson for her community.

Research fishing industry regulations. Create a presentation that explains how one or more of these regulations are intended to help preserve biodiversity in a marine or freshwater ecosystem.

☐ Technology Connection

Signal Transformation Information transfer technologies often receive one type of signal and change it into another. For example, a radio receives electromagnetic radio wave signals and transforms them into electric signals. Speakers convert the electric signals into sound waves in the air.

Conduct research to learn how an information technology you use daily converts signals from one form to another, and summarize what you learn in a well-written paragraph. Explain how engineers designed the device to minimize loss of signal clarity while performing signal transformations.

☐ Life Science Connection

Frogs and Pollution Frogs and other amphibians respire through their skins, so they are some of the most sensitive animals to pollution in the environment. Frog and toad species across the world are in danger of extinction because of pollution.

Research the effects of pollution on different species of frogs, toads, or salamanders. Explain the effects the pollution has on the amphibian and its environment. Create a poster or visual display that explains how frogs or other amphibians can be used to monitor the effects of resource use on Earth's systems.

Name: _____   Date: _____

Use the graph to answer Questions 1–4.

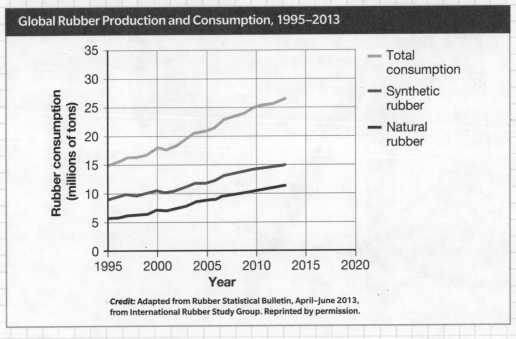

Global Rubber Production and Consumption, 1995–2013

Credit: Adapted from Rubber Statistical Bulletin, April–June 2013, from International Rubber Study Group. Reprinted by permission.

1. What trend can you see in the graph in the consumption of natural and synthetic rubber between 1995 and 2013?

2. What might account for the trend? Explain your reasoning.

3. How does this trend in rubber consumption affect Earth's systems?

4. Based on what you know about human population change, how would you expect the consumption of natural rubber and synthetic rubber to change in the future? How might this change affect Earth's systems? Use evidence and scientific reasoning to justify your claims.

Use the compact disc diagram to answer Questions 5–8.

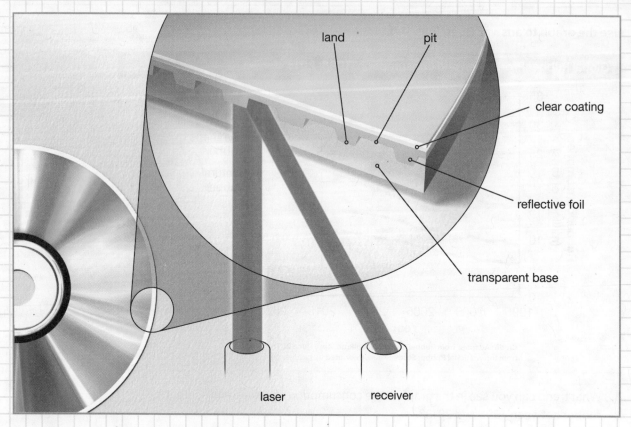

5. What evidence presented in the diagram shows that the compact disc is a form of digital storage?

6. How does the use of light to "read" the pits and lands minimize noise in comparison to a needle "reading" the groove on a vinyl record?

7. What big ideas about waves did engineers need to know to develop CD technology?

8. Music is increasingly stored digitally and accessed remotely through the Internet. How does this situation compare with storing and accessing music locally on a CD?

Name: _____   Date: _____

How does population change affect energy consumption in Japan?

Since 1990, Japan's population growth has slowed significantly, and the nation's population began to decline after 2010. However, Japan's electrical energy consumption remains high, especially in rural areas. You have been asked to explain these trends to Japanese energy officials. Research how energy is generated and used in Japan, in Japan's cities, and in rural Japan. You may need to evaluate population change and demographics, regional differences in energy use, and per capita use. Present your findings as a multimedia presentation, animation, flow chart, or series of if-then statements that explains the patterns of population change and energy use in Japan.

Population Change and Electricity Consumption in Japan and in Rural Japan

The first figure shows the changes in population and electrical energy use for all of Japan. The second figure shows the same information for rural areas of Japan.

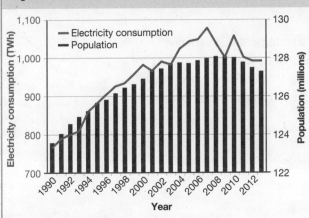
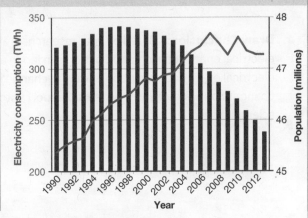

Credit: Adapted from "Population decline and electricity demand in Japan" by Akira Yanagisawa, from IEE Japan, June 2015. Reprinted by permission.

The steps below will help guide your research and help you draw conclusions.

1. **Ask a Question** Write a question that defines the problem you have been asked to solve. You may also want to list questions you have about population change and energy consumption in Japan. These questions may help guide your research.

2. **Conduct Research** How do people in Japan use energy? What type of resources do they use to generate electricity? How does the use of these resources affect Earth systems? What social or technological trends might affect how electrical energy is used in rural areas and in urban areas?

3. **Analyze the Data** Use the information you gathered to identify proportional relationships between population change, per capita use, and resource use in Japan. Describe the proportional relationships between the three variables, and identify how those patterns can be used to predict changes in electrical energy use in Japan.

4. **Draw Conclusions** Based on your research, draft a statement that explains electrical energy consumption patterns in Japan and makes predictions about how electrical energy consumption is likely to change in Japan's future and how those changes could affect Earth systems. Support your claim by using evidence and scientific reasoning.

5. **Communicate** Present your findings to the board of energy officials in Japan. Use words and images to explain to them what has caused the energy consumption in Japan to remain high despite the drop in population.

✓ **Self-Check**

	I asked a question about how energy consumption relates to population change and trends in energy use.
	I researched how energy is used in Japan, and how societal trends affect energy use and Earth Systems.
	I identified relationships between population change, per capita use, and energy use in Japan and used this information to make a claim.
	My conclusion was clearly stated and communicated to others.

Go online to access the **Interactive Glossary**. You can use this online tool to look up definitions for all the vocabulary terms in this book.

Pronunciation Key

Sound	Symbol	Example	Respelling	Sound	Symbol	Example	Respelling
ă	a	pat	PAT	ŏ	ah	bottle	BAHT'l
ā	ay	pay	PAY	ō	oh	toe	TOH
âr	air	care	KAIR	ô	aw	caught	KAWT
ä	ah	father	FAH•ther	ôr	ohr	roar	ROHR
är	ar	argue	AR•gyoo	oi	oy	noisy	NOYZ•ee
ch	ch	chase	CHAYS	o͞o	u	book	BUK
ĕ	e	pet	PET	o͞o	oo	boot	BOOT
ĕ (at end of a syllable)	eh	settee lessee	seh•TEE leh•SEE	ou	ow	pound	POWND
ĕr	ehr	merry	MEHR•ee	s	s	center	SEN•ter
ē	ee	beach	BEECH	sh	sh	cache	CASH
g	g	gas	GAS	ŭ	uh	flood	FLUHD
ĭ	i	pit	PIT	ûr	er	bird	BERD
ĭ (at end of a syllable)	ih	guitar	gih•TAR	z	z	xylophone	ZY•luh•fohn
ī	y eye (only for a complete syllable)	pie island	PY EYE•luhnd	z	z	bags	BAGZ
îr	ir	hear	HIR	zh	zh	decision	dih•SIZH•uhn
j	j	germ	JERM	ə	uh	around broken focus	uh•ROWND BROH•kuhn FOH•kuhs
k	k	kick	KIK	ər	er	winner	WIN•er
ng	ng	thing	THING	th	th	thin they	THIN THAY
ngk	ngk	bank	BANGK	w	w	one	WUHN
				wh	hw	whether	HWETH•er

Index

Page numbers for key terms are in **boldface** type.
Page numbers in *italic* type indicate illustrative material, such as photographs, graphs, charts, and maps.

A

Abell-370 galaxy cluster, *291*
absolute age, 16, 320–322, 348
absolute dating, 320, 322
absorption, 505
absorption of wave, 505–506, 507
acanthostega, *352*
acceleration, 55
  effect of collision during, 106
  friction effect on, 79, 84
  rate of velocity changes, 76
  in relationship to mass, 81–85
  speed's relationship to, 55
  unbalanced forces changing,
    77–80, 97, *97*
acid rain, 603
acoustic panel, 512, *512*
acquired trait, 396
Act, 9, 79, 217, 241, 246, 532, 643
action force, 86–88, 96
adaptations, 427
  of cactus and their predator, 409,
    409
  evolution of, 398
  identifying, 428, *428*
  of manta rays, 394, *394*
  of predator, 399–403, 409, *409*
  of rafflesia flowers, *395*
  traits for organism survival,
    427–428
adenine (A), 419, *419*
adenoviruses, 464, *464*
African elephant, 378–379, *378*
agriculture
  changes in land used for, 608, *608*
  population growth rate affected by,
    573, *573*
air, light traveling through, 518–519
airbag, 80, *80*
airplane, 478, *478*
air resistance, 193, 196
algae, 391
allele, 437, *437*, 442, *442*

allele frequency, 405
alpaca, 435, *435*, 449, *449*, 576, *576*,
  589, *589*
alphadon, *357*, *357*
Altamira, Brazil, 592, *592*
Alvarez, Luis, 8, *8*, 11
Alvarez, Walter, 8, *8*, 11, 15
amber, 336, *336*
ambulocetus natans, 353, *353*, 370,
  370
American badger, 308, *308*
amino acid chain, 420, *420*, 421, *421*
ammeter, 134, 139, 155–158, *155*, *156*
ammonites
  in ancient sea, 311, *311*, 325, *325*
  index fossil of, 318
amphibian, evolution of, 352, *352*
amplitude, 489
amplitude of waves
  energy of partial reflection and, *508*
  of light wave, 522, *522*, 539
  modulating, 626, *626*
  volume relating to, 506, *506*
  as wave property, 489–492
  wave size affected by, 504–506,
    515, *515*
anacus, *379*
analog information, 622, *622*
analog signal, 623
  analyzing, 621–625
  compared to digital signal, 565
  continuous information, 623–624,
    623, 637
  converting to digital, 628
  modulating, 626–627
  noise affecting, *629*, 631, *631*, 637,
    644
  storage of, 632, *632*
analysis
  of apparent motion of the sun, 217
  of correlation, 20
  of Earth, moon, and sun system,
    242

  of Earth's tilt, 550
  of Earth-Sun model, 549–554
  of electrical force, 127, 129, 130–131
  of electromagnet, 153
  of encoding messages, 617
  of energy, 28–31
  of energy in systems, 43–44
  of extinction and land use, 608
  of extinction data, 356
  of factors in resource use, 580
  of falling objects, 186
  of forces, 58–61, 83
  of fossil record, 358–359
  of fossil to describe Earth's past,
    314
  of gravitational forces, 188
  of growth curve data, 376, *376*
  of impact of water use, 598
  of inferences from evidence, 377
  of kinetic and potential energy,
    35–38
  of law of universal gravitation, 258
  of light transmission, 531
  of longitudinal and transverse
    waves, 487
  of magnets, 143, 144–145, 146–147
  of mechanical waves generation,
    501
  of the moon's craters, 16
  of motion of falling objects, 195
  of observations, 289
  of other galaxies, 291–296
  of packing materials, 103–104
  of parallax, 224
  of population growth and resource
    use, 577–578
  of protein folding, 422
  of rock layers, 317, 334
  of salamander species distribution,
    401–402
  of selected traits in vegetables,
    438–439
  of signal, 630
  of solar system model, 281–282

fossil record (continued)

evidence of changes over time, 397

evidence of Earth's past, 310–322, 333, 365

finding absolute age, 320–322, 327

geologic time scale of, 321, *321*

index fossil, 318

inference from, 360, *360*

in Carnegie Quarry, *314*

in Chicxulub Crater, 16

in Morrison Formation, 314

patterns in, 6–9, 25, *359*

in Republic of Madagascar, 307, *307*

uniformitarianism in interpreting, 315

updating, 7

of whole animals, *314*

Foucault, Leon, 251–252, *251, 252*

frequency, 491

frequency modulated (FM) radio, 626

frequency of wave

absorption and, 506, *506*

energy of electromagnetic wave depends on, 521

of light wave, 522–523, *522, 539*

modulating, 626, *626*

reflection and, 508, *508*

in relationship to energy, *491*

sun emitting many different, 522, *522*

friction

astronauts lacking, 86, *86*

first law of motion and, 79

force of, 60

of maglev trains, 209–210

second law of motion and, 84

thermal energy from, 79

wave losing energy to, 506

frog, 660, *660*

full moon, 243, *243*

G

Galápagos island, 397, *397, 410, 410*

galaxy, 284

amount of, 286, *286*

analyzing other, 291–296

clusters of, 294

defined by shape, 293, *293*

model of, 278, 284–286

orbits of, 198

universe full of, 295, *295*

Galileo Galilei, 227, 288, *288*

gamma ray, 268, 520, *520*

Ganymede, 22, *22,* 228

Garza, Dolly, 660, *660*

gardener, 434, *43*

gas planet, 260

Gemini, 220, *220*

gene, 419

artificial selection not changing, 443

from both parents, 419, *419*

changes in causing color change, 417, *417,* 431, *431*

codes for proteins, 420, *420,* 454, *454*

combination of from parents, 368

for fur color, 416, *416,* 423

identifying function of through knockout mice, 461, *461*

mutation of, 424–428, 433

OCA2 and HER2, 454, *454*

relationship with traits, 418–423

as segments of DNA, 419, 433, 454, *454*

suicide gene, 464, *464*

gene insertion, 454–459, *454*

gene modification

of chickens, 462, *462*

of crops, 454–455, *454, 460, 460*

impact of, 466, *466*

influencing traits in populations, 458–459

for insulin production, 459, *459*

of mice, 461, *461*

milestones in, 456

of mosquitoes, 461, *461*

for pharmaceutical purposes, 462, *462*

of sexually reproducing organisms, 458, *458*

gene therapy, 464–466, **464,** *464,* 471, *471*

genetically modified crop, 454–455, *454, 460*

genetically modified organism (GMO), 460, *460, 471, 471*

genetic engineering, 454

artificial selection compared to, 455

bioethics of, 467–468

biotechnology of, 454–459

changing genes with, 443

evaluating, 452

modeling of, 457–458, *457*

techniques of, 454–459, 471, *471*

geneticist, 472

genetic material

of banana crop, 392, *392*

changes in over generations, 398

DNA, 368, 418–423

genetic mutation

causes of, 424–426, *424*

causing blue lobsters, 417, *417,* 431, *431*

for natural selection, 399

relationship to natural selection, 427–428, 433

from UV rays, 426, *426*

genetic variation

causes of, 404

causing different traits, 406

natural selection of, 398–403

of phenotypes, 406

relating distribution of traits to, 404–406

genotype, 405, 439

geocentric solar system model, 222, *222,* 223–226, *223*

geologic change, rate of, 330–331

geologic time scale, 336

detail on, 336

division of, 321, *321,* 339

evidence used for, 329, *329,* 343, *343*

of increasing complexity of life, 351, *351*

organizing Earth's past, 328–340, 345

reconstructing, 6

geologists

analyzing rock layers, 334, *334*

dating rock layers, 16, 349

relative dating of rock layers, 318

geosphere

as subsystem of Earth, 592

impact of using resources from, 602–605

© Houghton Mifflin Harcourt Publishing Company

mass (continued)

gravitational force of, 173

gravity affected by, 187, 189–191, 258

impact crater based on, 262

inertia in relationship to, 80

kinetic energy dependent on, 35–37, 49

measurement of, 184–185

on the moon, 184, *184*

relationship with acceleration, force, and, 85

shape of space objects relative to, 259, *259*

of sun, 200

mass extinction

causes of, 20, *20*, 25

defined, 7–8

fossil record recording, 6, 354–355

hypothesis of, 9, 19

mastodon, 379

mastodon tooth, 378, *378*

Math Connection

Leap Year, 302

mathematical laws, 189

mathematical models

of planets, 230

of solar system, 226, 229, 280

of sound wave, 560

matter

attracted to other matter, 189–191

interactions with light, 529–534

light refracted by, 532–534

light transmitting through, 530–531

reflecting light by, *529*

in solar system, 198

solar system formed by, 256–272

wave interacting with, 498–510

wave medium, 482, 500, *500*

Mauna Loa Observatory, 604, *604*

measurement

of current, 157

of distance using brightness, 295

of light reflection, 536

light year, 284

of work, 28

mechanical energy, defined, 30

mechanical wave, 500

absorption of, 505–506, *505*

generating, 501–502, 515

partial transmission, 509

reflection of, 508–509, *508*

sea floor maps generated by, 499, *499*, 513, *513*

spreading out of, 505

types of, 500–503, *502*

medicine, 573, *573*

medium, 482

medium ground finch, 410, *410*

medium or media (of wave), 482

behaviors of waves at boundaries of, 507–510, 515, *515*

refraction and, 533, *533*

speed of light through, 519, *519*

types of, 500, *500*

wave speed dependent on, 503, *503*

meganeura, 360, *360*

melanin, in eye color, 454, *454*

Mendel, Gregor, 437, *437*, 441

Mercury

comparing to other space objects, *232*

composition of, 260

density of, *260*

Firdousi Crater on, 262, *262*

gravity of, *258*

movement of, 221

scale model of, *280*

metal, 576

metaspriggina, 351, *351*

meteor

energy of, 30, *30*, 49, *49*

Meteor Crater, Arizona, 96, *96*

meteorite

absolute age of, 322

composition of, 271, *271*

rate of geologic change from, 330–331

rocks recording, 312

scale of, 230–231, *230–231*

metric system

gram (g), 184

kilogram (kg), 184

micrograph, of drug-resistant bacteria, 429, *429*

microscopic marine life, 16

microwave, 30, 520, *520*

Milky Way

counting stars in, 285

early theories of, 287, 288

Earth's place in, 290, 299, *299*

galaxy, *287*

galaxy of, 212, *212*, 278, *278*, 284–286, 301

map of, 288

model of, 279, *279*, 287–290

motion of stars in, 183, *183*, 203, *203*

shape of, 288

size of, 284–285

Mimas, Herschel Crater, 262, *262*

mineral, 602

mining, 602

mirror, 529, *529*

model

of asteroid impact, 42, *42*

of change, 394

of Earth, moon, and sun system, 241–242

of Earth-sun-model, 549–554, *549*

Earth's tilt, 550, *550*

factors in resource use, 580

of fields, 171–172, 181

of fossil formation, 310

genetic basis for artificial selection, 441–443

genetic modification of bacteria, 457–458, *457*

of light as wave, 516–534

of light wave, 522–524, 539

of longitudinal and transverse waves, 486–487

of Milky Way, 212, *212*, 279, *279*, 287–290

of natural selection, 398–403

nebular disk formation, 265–266

of noncontact forces, 166–169

of objects' behaviors, 32, *32*

of properties of waves, 489–492

of protein folding, 421–422

of relationship between population and resource use, 577–578

of relative age, 316–317

of solar and lunar eclipses, 245

of solar system, 222–225

© Houghton Mifflin Harcourt Publishing Company

© Houghton Mifflin Harcourt Publishing Company